JAVA™
MODELING
in COLOR
with UML®

ISBN 0-13-011510-X

9 780130 115102

90000

JAVA™
MODELING
in COLOR
with UML®

Enterprise Components and Process

Peter Coad

Eric Lefebvre

Jeff De Luca

To subscribe to the Coad Letter®, visit:
www.oi.com

Prentice Hall PTR
Upper Saddle River, NJ 07458
http://www.phptr.com

Library of Congress Cataloging-in-Publication Data
Coad, Peter.
    Java modeling in color with UML : enterprise components and
process / Peter Coad, Eric Lefebvre, Jeff De Luca.
        p.   cm.
    Includes bibliographical references and index.
    ISBN 0-13-011510-X
    1. Java (Computer program language) 2. UML (Computer science)
I. Lefebvre, Eric. II. De Luca, Jeff. III. Title.
QA76.73.J38C652 1999
005.13'3--dc21

Editorial/Production Supervision: *Precision Graphics*
Acquisitions Editor: *Jeffrey Pepper*
Editorial Assistant: *Linda Ramagnano*
Marketing Manager: *Dan Rush*
Cover Design: *Anthony Gemmellaro*
Cover Design Direction: *Jerry Votta*
Manufacturing Manager: *Alexis R. Heydt*
Project Coordinator: *Anne Trowbridge*

Published by Prentice Hall PTR
Prentice-Hall, Inc.
Upper Saddle River, NJ 07458

The Coad Letter® is a registered trademark of Object International. Together® is a
registered trademark of Object International Software.
Post-it® is a registered trademark of 3M.
UML® is a registered trademark of the Object Management Group. Unified
Modeling Language® is a trademark of the Object Management Group.

The book, tour and lightbulb icons are from The Learning Company and are used with
its permission. © 1998 The Learning Company, Inc. and its licensors.

Prentice Hall books are widely used by corporations and government agencies for
training, marketing, and resale.

The publisher offers discounts on this book when ordered in bulk
quantities. For more information, contact Corporate Sales Department,
phone: 800-382-3419; fax: 201-236-7141; e-mail: corpsales@prenhall.com
or write:

Prentice Hall PTR
Corporate Sales Department
One Lake Street
Upper Saddle River, NJ 07458

Printed in the United States of America
10 9 8 7 6 5 4 3 2

ISBN 0-13-011510-X

Prentice-Hall International (UK) Limited, *London*
Prentice-Hall of Australia Pty. Limited, *Sydney*
Prentice-Hall Canada Inc., *Toronto*
Prentice-Hall Hispanoamericana, S.A., *Mexico*
Prentice-Hall of India Private Limited, *New Delhi*
Prentice-Hall of Japan, Inc., *Tokyo*
Prentice-Hall (Singapore) Pte. Ltd., *Singapore*
Editora Prentice-Hall do Brasil, Ltda., *Rio de Janeiro*

From Peter Coad

To Judy, David, Amy, and Ben

From Eric Lefebvre

To André Malo, for his constant and friendly support

From Jeff De Luca

To Michelle, Matthew, and Catherine

Contents

Preface

Archetypes, color, and components will forever change how you build Java models. We build Java models with teams of developers. In our day-to-day mentoring, we develop and try out new ideas and innovations that will help those developers excel at modeling. Some of those ideas fall by the wayside. Some provide modest help. Others, according to our clients, are home runs. In this book, we reveal some of our home runs.

Chapter 1 explores the importance of color and introduces the color-coding that project teams have been applying with success around the globe. It also introduces the domain-neutral component, a template that you'll see applied again and again in the chapters that follow.

Chapters 2–5 deliver ready-to-use Java models. These chapters present 61 domain-specific components, each one an interesting teaching by example. Use the components as they are, extend them with plug-ins, extend them by adding your own content, or use them as an outside opinion (comparing and contrasting with your own ongoing work).

Chapter 6 delivers a process that integrates Java modeling into the delivery of frequent, tangible, working results.

We hope you enjoy this new material!

Peter Coad (pc@oi.com)
Eric Lefebvre (lefee@groupe-progestic.com)
Jeff De Luca (jdl@nebulon.com)

ACKNOWLEDGMENTS

This book would not be in your hands without the kind help of many people. We especially thank:

- Our clients, who have allowed us to develop this material in practice first, where it really counts—with special thanks to clients in Durham, Columbus (Ohio), Hartford, Montreal, Oslo, and Singapore,

- Jon Kern, for his many insights, suggestions, and tireless effort, improving the technical content of this book,

- Mark Mayfield and David North, for their collaboration with Peter on a predecessor to this work, *Object Models: Strategies, Patterns, and Applications,*

- David Taylor, for reading an early manuscript and sharing his thoughts with us, raising questions that would have otherwise gone unanswered,

- Phil Bradley, for gently nudging us into expanding the domain-neutral component into an overall template, as well as advocating "archetype" over other terms we considered,

- Barbara Hanscome, Editor-in-Chief at *Software Development* magazine, for encouraging us to gain a deeper understanding of the color theory,

- Roger Thompson at OCLC for pointing us to the Root-Bernstein article on visual thinking,

- John Gage at Sun Microsystems for encouraging Jeff to begin writing about what we now refer to as feature-driven development,

- Stephen Palmer for his collaboration during the development of feature-driven development,

- M. A. Rajashima for introducing us to the "entry criteria, tasks, verification, and exit criteria" approach,

- Lim Bak Wee at United Overseas Bank for introducing us to progress-reporting in color,

- Jeffrey Pepper at Prentice Hall for his encouragement and vision,

- The production team at Precision Graphics for their significant talent in transforming our manuscript into the book you now hold in your hands.

We also thank those who provided technical feedback during the development of this material, including: David Anderson, Håkan Axelsson, Tom Considine, Rikard Dahlman, Terry Gliedt, Low Heng Sin, Mike Morrison, Ajay Kumar Rana, R. Mark Sharp, Paul Szego, and Julia Tan.

This book would not have been possible without some rather remarkable UML-in-color modeling software. We hereby acknowledge and thank our friends, the Together/J team members, with special thanks to Dietrich Charisius (Chief Architect), Alexander Aptus, Sergey Dmitriev, Valentin Kipyatkov, Igor Bazarny, Andrei Ivanov, Kate Gorentchuk, Fyodor Isakov, Eugene Belyaev, Konstantin Savvin, Robert Palomo, Maxim Livov, Frank Baker, Lee Youngblood, Robert Neher, Frank Sterkmann, and Hanspeter Siegrist.

About the Authors

Peter Coad (pronounced "code") is the lead author of the first book to integrate color and enterprise components into a model-building approach. Peter is one of the world's most experienced model builders (many hundreds of models in nearly every industry imaginable). His current consulting practice focuses on Java-inspired modeling for building better enterprise-wide applications. His company, Object International, delivers workshops, mentoring, and software, "helping teams deliver frequent, tangible, working results."

pc@oi.com
www.oi.com

Eric Lefebvre (pronounced "leh-fay'-vreh") has spent many years developing enterprise-wide models, with special emphasis on building generic models, along with developing methods, techniques, and tools for reusing generic models. He is the Director of Research at Progestic Group in Montreal, Canada, an IT consulting firm of about 300 professionals.

lefee@groupe-progestic.com
www.groupe-progestic.com

Jeff De Luca is a technology-savvy project manager, one Peter Coad describes as "the best project manager I've ever worked with." The technical side of Jeff's skills is in developing enterprise-wide and system-wide architectures. His consulting practice, Nebulon Pty Ltd, is an information technology consulting and publishing firm, currently specializing in management consulting, architecture, and Java development.

jdl@nebulon.com
www.nebulon.com

Archetypes, Color, and the Domain-Neutral Component

▶ Pink: It's my favorite crayon.

Aerosmith

Black-and-white conveys basic information. Color reaches out and *grabs* you.

Just as the transition from black-and-white photography to color is so profound, the transition from black-and-white modeling to color is an awesome one.

Welcome to the world of modeling in color, with archetypes, a domain-neutral component, and 61 domain-specific components.

In this chapter, you'll learn and apply archetypes, color, and the domain-neutral component. In Chapters 2–5, you'll read and apply a wide variety of domain-specific components. In Chapter 6, you'll discover feature-driven development, the process for putting all of this into best practice.

How does Java fit in? Many of the model shapes are Java inspired. You'll find composition rather than inheritance. You'll also see a judicious use of interface plug-in points—for added flexibility. In addition, the CD includes all of the models plus Java skeleton source code, ready for "design by feature, build by feature" expansion, as described in Chapter 6.

We've developed this book as a front-end companion to *Java Design*. That book delivers specific strategies for designing with composition, designing with threads, and designing with notification.

Throughout this book, we use Unified Modeling Language (UML) notation. The class-diagram notation and conventions we use in this book are shown in Figure 1-1. The sequence-diagram notation and conventions we use are shown in Figure 1-2. We suggest you scan those figures now, then refer back to them from time to time.

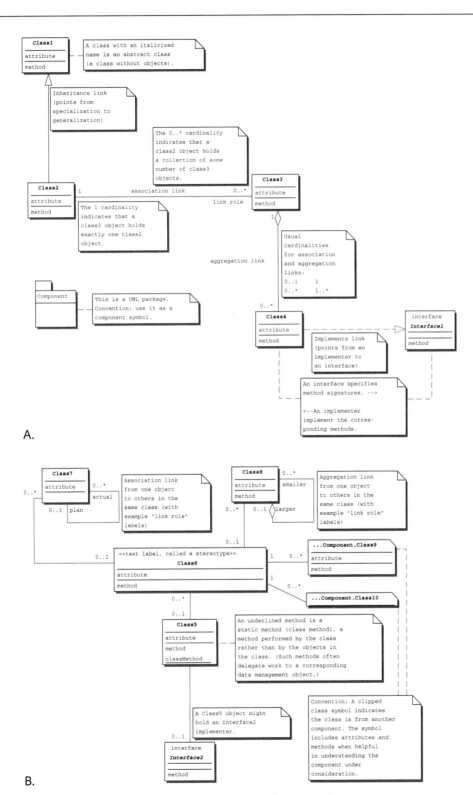

FIGURE 1-1 ▲ Class-diagram notation and conventions.

▲ 1

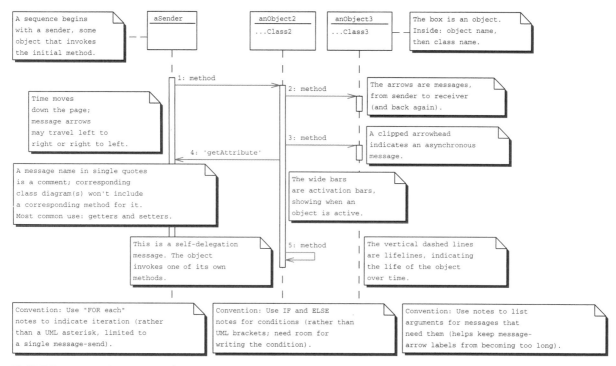

FIGURE 1-2. ▲ Sequence-diagram notation and conventions

1.1 ARCHETYPES

Now let's turn our attention to this chapter's first major topic: archetypes. Here's the concept we want to communicate:

A form or template for one of a small number of class categories. It specifies attributes, links, methods, plug-in points, and interactions that are typical for classes in that category.

Which of the following is the better term for this concept?

Stereotype

1. An unvarying model, as though cast from a mold
2. A text tag for annotating a UML diagram element
3. A broad categorization of classes

Archetype

A form from which all things of the same kind *more or less* follow.

[DERIVED FROM WEBSTER75 AND HAYAKAWA68]

It's a fact. "Archetype" says it best. An archetype is a form from which all classes of the same kind *more or less* follow—including attributes, links, methods, plug-in points, and interactions.[1]

Yet which archetypes prove most useful in building better models?

We've developed hundreds of models in dozens of business and engineering domains. Along the way, we continually looked for ways to "abstract up" to a domain-neutral component—a small model of archetypes that we could apply again and again in our workshops and mentoring assignments. Why? We felt we could teach more in less time and accomplish more in less time. Better for our clients, more interesting for us, win-win.

Over time, we've discovered four interconnected archetypes that form a domain-neutral component:

1. The moment-interval archetype
2. The role archetype
3. The "catalog-entry-like description" archetype
4. The "party, place or thing" archetype

We'd like to acknowledge that Peter Coad and Mark Mayfield laid the early groundwork for these four archetypes, first described in [Coad92] and later extended with David North in [Coad95–97].

1.1.1 The Moment-Interval Archetype

The first archetype in importance is a moment in time or an interval of time. It represents something that one needs to work with and track for business or legal reasons, something that occurs at a moment in time or over an interval of time. For short, we call it a "moment-interval" to help remind us that we are looking for either a moment or an interval of importance in the problem domain.

A sale is made at a moment in time—the date and time of that sale.

A rental happens over an interval of time, from checkout to return. A reservation occurs over an interval of time, from the time that it is made until the time it is used, canceled, or expires.

A sale could even be an interval of time, if you need to track the duration of the sales process itself, perhaps for performance assessment.

What's important is that you recognize it is one of these two, moment or interval, rather than which one of the two it is. So we establish it as one archetype, moment-interval.

---

[1] Archetypes are forms that are *more or less* followed. The "more or less" aspect is essential. In contrast, stereotypes are unvarying. Also in contrast, inheritance and interfaces specify names that must be followed rather than more or less followed.

1.1.1.1 Using Archetypes to Identify Classes and Much More

In any domain, one can look for moment-intervals and begin building a model. In material-resource management, we can move from request to RFQ to PO to delivery to invoice. In manufacturing management, we can move from a planned process and its steps to an actual process and its steps.

So one of the ways that archetypes help in guiding model building is in identifying classes that need to be included in the model.

Yet archetypes are more than simply a categorization of classes. They are also a categorization of the responsibilities (the attributes, links, methods, plug-in points, and interactions) that such classes usually have.

1.1.1.2 Labeling an Archetype

What we need is a text tag, so we can indicate which archetype we are applying when establishing a class. In UML, that text tag is called a stereotype, an extension mechanism within that notation (Figure 1-3).

The problem is that text tags like <<moment-interval>> hide some very important meaning in a rather plain and simple text label. In a family of diagrams, that little label is lost in the noise as it begins to look like all the other labels. And that is too bad; expressing the archetype is far more important than it would be getting credit for. It would be nice if one could give this added layer of information added punch, so it could:

- grab your attention to work on that part of the diagram first,
- help you discover a progression of moment-intervals over time,
- guide you in linking other classes into the moment-interval you are working with, and
- quietly move you to considering what is linked to that moment-interval and how it works with others to get things done.

Expressing archetypes with color is the extra dimension, the added punch that does all that and more.

1.1.1.3 Implementing Archetypes

What does an archetype look like in source code?

An archetype describes a model for classes within that archetype to more or less follow. It's the "more or less" aspect that is important here.

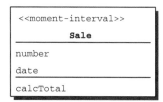

FIGURE 1-3. ▲ Using a UML text tag to indicate a moment-interval.

Could one implement an archetype as a superclass and then inherit from it? No! Here's why: The very nature of an archetype is that each and every class that follows an archetype only more or less follows it. Inheritance is far too rigid for what archetypes are all about, what they need to express.

The other way to implement an archetype is by using a keyword-coded comment, one that modeling tools can recognize and use effectively. In Java, we do this with a javadoc-style comment, using a coded keyword. For example, here's such a comment with an embedded keyword (following the @ symbol):

```
/** @archetype moment-interval*/
public class Sale {
 public BigDecimal calcTotal(){...
 }
 private int number;
 private Date date;
}
```

That gets the job done nicely.

1.1.2 The Role Archetype

The second archetype in importance is a role. A role is a way of participation by a person, place, or thing.

Another way to say this is that a role is a way of participation by a party (person or organization), place, or thing. We like this better, since many times a person or an organization is eligible to play the same role (for example, owner) within a problem domain that we are working in. Often, a moment-interval has parts, called moment-interval details. Think of them as being a little piece of a moment-interval, something it needs to do its job.

So we model the role player (a party, place, or thing) as well as the role (the "hat" that the party, place, or thing is wearing). The role player captures core attributes and behaviors that apply no matter what combination of hats it might be wearing. For person, that often includes attributes like legal name and date of birth. It also includes methods that enforce business rules across the collection of roles being played. For example, a method "authorized for" in a person object interacts with each role; then it applies rules across that collection of roles to determine if a person is authorized to take a given action (Figure 1-4).

Party, person, and organization roles are the norm. Occasionally you'll find place and thing roles too (for example, a product and its two roles, "product in a sales process" and "product in use").

1.1.3 The Description Archetype

The third archetype is a description. More specifically, it's a catalog-entry-like description. It is a collection of values that apply again and again. It

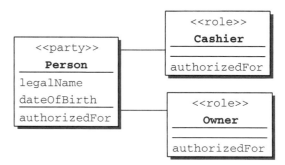

FIGURE 1-4. ▲ A party and its roles.

also provides behavior across the collection of all things that correspond to its description.

For example, your red pickup is a vehicle; it's a thing with its own serial number (called a vehicle identification number), purchase date, color, and odometer reading. The corresponding catalog-entry-like description is vehicle description; it establishes manufacturer, model number, date of manufacture, and available colors; it also is a good place to locate business-related methods like, "how many of these trucks are in good working order?"

1.1.4 The "Party, Place, or Thing" Archetype

A party (meaning a person or an organization), place, or thing is someone or something who plays different roles. A person might be both an employee and a customer. A place might be both a retail outlet and a wholesale outlet. A thing might play one role in a manufacturing process and a different role in a purchasing process.

1.2 COLOR

In September of 1997, we started building models with four colors of Post-it Notes: pink, yellow, green, and blue—one for each archetype. Developers and domain experts new to model building on the team commented a number of times along the way, "But how could you possibly build effective models without color?" That caught our attention! So we developed this technique in practice, published initial findings [Coad97a], and presented this approach in an OOPSLA '97 tutorial [Coad97b].

As is often the case, practice preceded theory. Seeing these ideas work so well in practice, we began investigating color and why it appears to have such a profound effect on building better models.

1.2.1 Why Use Color?

Why use color in component models? Color gives us a way to encode additional layers of information. The wise use of color increases the *amount of content* we can express.

More importantly, one can use color to add layers of new content to models. Those layers are visible from a distance, so that "big picture" model content comes across even before one starts reading the details. We call this effect "spatial layering;" it means that a model is capable of delivering an overview and a detailed view all within itself, without needing to break visual context by jumping to some other representation. Color makes spatial layering possible.

> Among the most powerful devices for reducing noise and enriching the content of displays is the technique of layering and separation, visually stratifying various aspects of the data. [He then describes how to do this: use distinctions in shape, lightness, size, and especially color.]
>
> EDWARD R. TUFTE [TUFTE90]

Hence, we can use color to enrich the content of models. In fact, we can apply color to achieve four objectives:

> The fundamental uses of color in information design: to label (color as a noun), to measure (color as a quantity), to represent or imitate reality (color as a representation), and to enliven or decorate (color as beauty).
>
> EDWARD R. TUFTE [TUFTE90]

What this means to modeling is that we can use color to:

- label added layers of information (for example, layers of classes with similar characteristics),
- indicate the progression of time (for example, one might use different shades of lightness to show such a progression),
- represent key categories of information within a model, and
- add visual impact to the model.

Added visual impact is important. Modeling is by its very nature a visually oriented activity. Those with strong spatial intelligence are especially drawn to model building and model reading.

> Spatial knowledge can serve a variety of scientific ends, a useful tool, an aid to thinking, a way of capturing information, a way of formulating problems, or the very means of solving the problem.
>
> HOWARD GARDNER [GARDNER83]

> This ability to idealize results, to see through the mess of real-life observations to what ought to be there, is one of the marks of genius.
>
> ROBERT SCOTT ROOT-BERNSTEIN [ROOT-BERNSTEIN85]

Adding color better engages the spatial intelligence of both model-builders and model-readers alike.

1.2.2 How Many Colors?

We started with four colors. Yet how many colors should we be using?

In visual design, it's a good idea to limit the number of colors in a color scheme. Why? Simply put: it's a good way to increase the likelihood of color harmony within that color scheme.

> Two or three colors is usually enough; five is too many. Four-color combinations must be selected with great care: nothing looks worse than too many colors, particularly when they lack common elements.
>
> HIDEAKI CHIJIIWA [CHIJIIWA87]

To support visual modeling in color, the last thing we want to do is end up with something that is visually distracting. We want to support better design, not distract from it. Hence, no matter how many semantic variations we might come up with, using four colors seems like a good place to start.

1.2.3 Which Colors?

The three-primary system, first proposed around 1731, defines primary colors as red, blue, and yellow. It defines secondary colors as orange, green, and violet.

The perceptual-primary system, first proposed by Leonardo da Vinci, defines primary colors as red, yellow, blue, and green. These are the perceptual primaries, those colors that do not appear to have any other color in them.

The six-primary system, first proposed in the 1990s, gives equal importance to red, yellow, green, blue, orange, and violet. The basis for this system is that blue and yellow don't make green; instead, bits of green impurities within so-called blue paint and so-called yellow paint make green. Hence green (and for that matter orange and violet) deserve to be considered primary colors too [Wilcox94].

We can mute these colors by adding a little white to them. That makes text placed on those colors much easier to read. So, for the four archetypes, we can use pink, pastel yellow, pastel blue, and pastel green. Let's see how!

1.3 THE FOUR ARCHETYPES IN COLOR

Our models always consist of four archetypes: role, moment-interval, thing, and description.

Let's match up archetypes with colors, to deliver that added impact we're looking for.

Moment-intervals tie together a component model. They express the heart and soul of what that component is all about. They usually have parts, called moment-interval details. In a model, moment-intervals often encapsulate the most interesting methods. Let's make moment-intervals pink, the most attention-grabbing of the colors.

Roles played are next when it comes to interesting responsibilities; we give them the next most attention-grabbing color, yellow. Parties, places, and things are next; we give them the next color in attention-grabbing, green. Descriptions usually have fairly simple responsibilities; we give then the calmest color of the four, blue (see Figure 1-5).

Each of these four colors corresponds to an archetype's characteristics: the attributes, links, methods, plug-in points, and interactions that corresponding classes more or less follow.

An archetype's characteristics include attributes and links as shown in Figure 1-6. A blue description knows its type, description, item number, and default value(s). A green party, place, or thing knows its serial number, name, address, and custom value(s). A yellow role knows its assigned number and status. A pink moment-interval knows its number, date (or date-time or interval), its priority, its total, and its status. A pink moment-interval detail knows its quantity.

Note the links, from blue to green to yellow to pink. In addition, usually, a pink moment-interval links to little pink moment-interval details. And sometimes a pink moment-interval links to planned or actual pink moment-interval(s).

You can tailor each blue-green-yellow-pink sequence you work with, customizing according to the level of specificity you need. Here's how. Include blue if you have groupings of values that apply again and again. Include green if you must track parties, places, or things individually

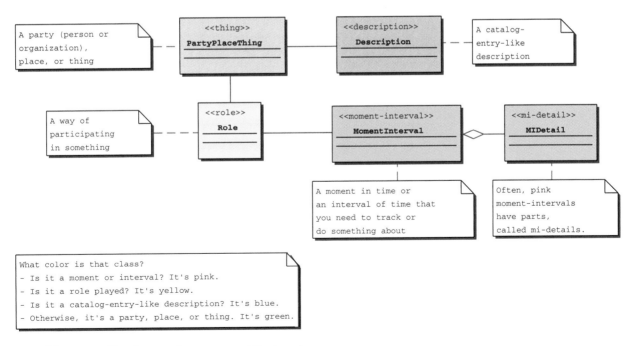

FIGURE 1-5. ▲ The four archetypes and their colors.

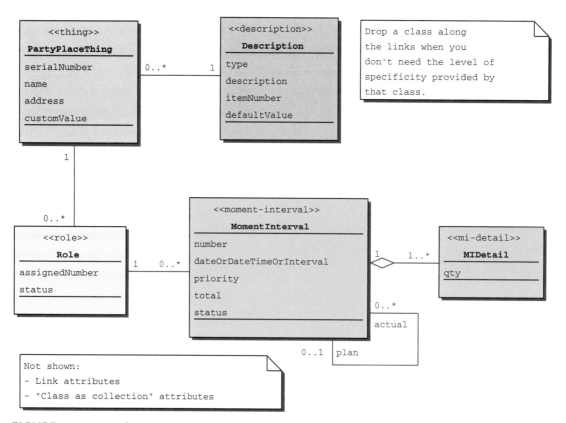

FIGURE 1-6. ▲ Archetypes—and their attributes and links.

rather than by quantity. Include yellow if you have role-specific responsibilities. Include pink if you need to remember the corresponding moment in time or interval of time.

An archetype's characteristics include methods (Figure 1-7). A blue description assesses across its corresponding green parties, places, or things; finds available; calculates quantity available; calculates total for a detail (with quantity and unit of measure); and lists its corresponding parties, places, or things. It also has static class-level methods (underlined, with behavior across all the objects in the class) to list all descriptions and to assess across all descriptions.

A green party, place, or thing assesses across its corresponding yellow roles; gets its custom value or, if not present, asks its corresponding blue description for its default value and returns it as its own; and lists its associated roles. Class-level methods list and assess across all parties, places, or things in the class.

A yellow role assesses across and lists its corresponding pink moment-intervals. At the class level, it lists all roles and assesses across all objects in the class.

A pink moment-interval makes one (supports the business process for making one, that is), adds details (parts), and calculates its total (interacting with its parts to do so). It can also recalculate its total (forcing a

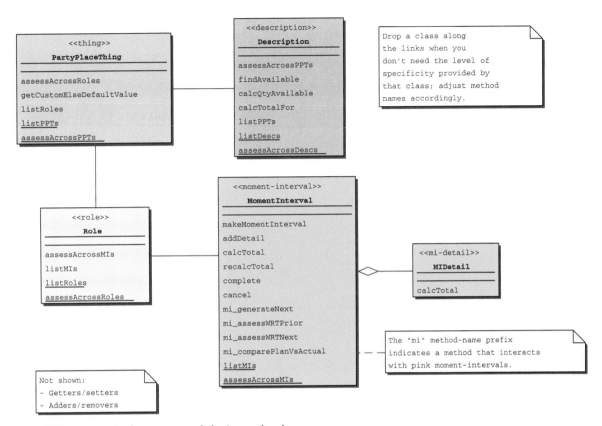

FIGURE 1-7. ▲ Archetypes and their methods.

recalculation, regardless of any internally buffered value). It accepts messages asking it to complete or cancel the moment-interval. It also provides behavior across other pink moment-intervals (designated by the prefix "mi_"): generate next, assess with respect to prior moment-intervals, assess with respect to next moment-intervals, and compare plan vs. actual. It also has two class-level methods: list all and assess across all. And each pink moment-interval detail calculates its total.

Note that we tend to list method names this way:

1. Make—the business-process method for a pink moment-interval
2. Calculate, assess, and the like
3. List
4. Moment-interval ("mi") methods (when a pink interacts with other pinks)
5. Class (static) methods, ones that apply across all of the objects in a class (such methods are underlined)

An archetype's characteristics include plug-in points for adapting the behavior of an archetype (Figure 1-8). A blue description needs a plug-in point when it has algorithmically complex behavior and we want the option

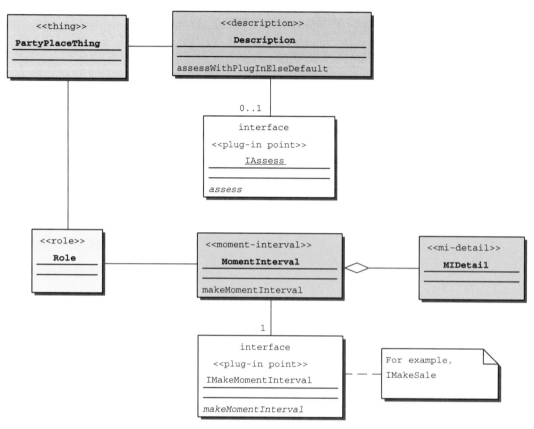

FIGURE 1-8. ▲ Archetypes and their plug-in points.

of plugging in an alternative behavior at times (IAssess, for example, ICalcInterest). A pink moment-interval needs a plug-in point whenever the business process is complicated enough that we really should design in plug-in flexibility to accommodate (anticipated or unanticipated) business process change over time (IMakeMomentInterval, for example, IMakeSale with a "one click" or a "shopping cart" plug-in).

Figure 1-9 summarizes the attributes, links, methods, and plug-in points of archetypes. We add interactions later in this chapter.

1.4 GIVEN A CLASS, WHAT'S THE COLOR, WHAT'S THE ARCHETYPE?

So given a class, what archetype or color should you use? Use this checklist:

1. Is it a moment in time or an interval of time, something the system needs to track for business or for legal reasons? If so, it's a pink moment-interval.
2. Otherwise, is it a role? If so, it's a yellow role.

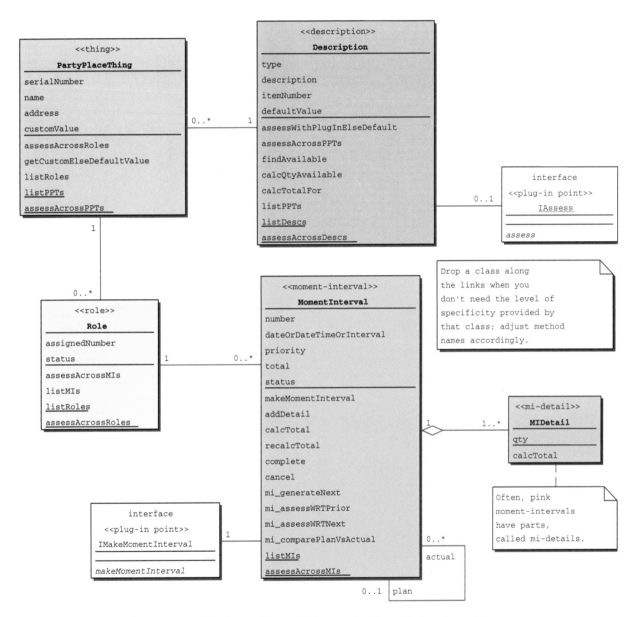

FIGURE 1-9. ▲ Archetypes and their attributes, links, methods, and plug-in points.

3. Otherwise, is it a catalog-like description, a grouping of values that you can apply again and again? If so, it's a blue description.

4. Otherwise, it's a party, place, or thing. It's a green party, place, or thing (green is the default; if not pink, yellow, or blue, it's green).

We also use white occasionally, for notes, for plug-in points, and for system-interaction proxies.

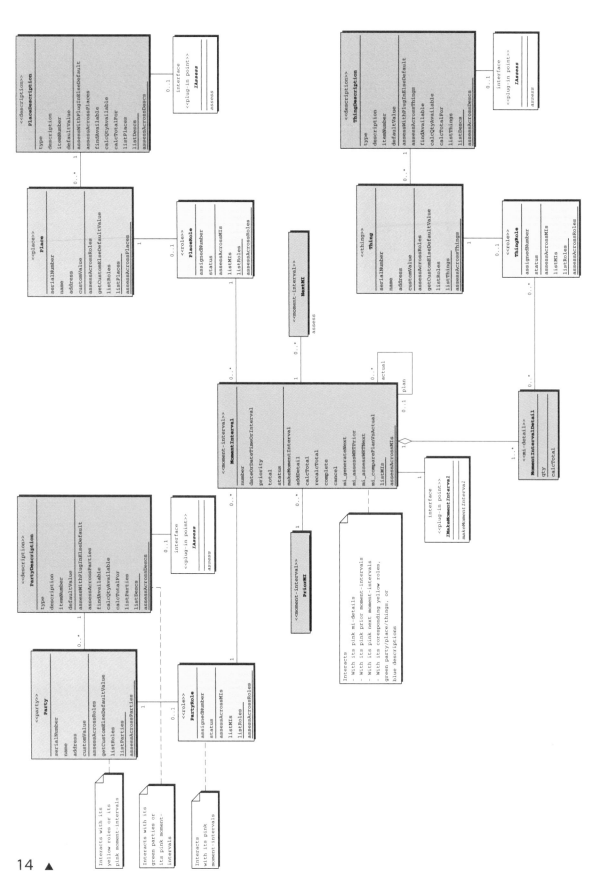

FIGURE 1-10. ▲ The domain-neutral component.

1.5 THE DOMAIN-NEUTRAL COMPONENT

Archetypes in color are very useful little building blocks.

Let's take them a step further.

These four archetypes in color plug into each other in a very repeatable and predictable way. We call it a "domain-neutral component."

We've built hundreds and hundreds of models. All of them follow this domain-neutral component model. In Chapters 2–5, you'll find 61 domain-specific components. All of them follow the domain-neutral component shown in Figure 1-10.

1.6 INTERACTIONS WITHIN THE DOMAIN-NEUTRAL COMPONENT

This section focuses on archetype interactions within the domain-neutral component.

Some refer to class diagrams as static and sequence diagrams as dynamic. Actually, neither diagram moves! It takes some imagination, some additional internal visualization, to see the motion.

Class diagrams are *implicitly* dynamic. (It takes a bit of imagination to see the interactions, although one really can learn to see them!) Sequence diagrams are *explicitly* dynamic (well, as good as it gets without having on-screen simulations in front of you).

Archetypes include typical interactions too. Once you know those interactions, even class diagrams spring to life.

Now rest assured, this is not an excuse for not including sequence diagrams in this book! Actually, you will find an equal balance of sequence diagrams and class diagrams in here.

We feel compelled to make this added point though, that with archetype interactions you really *can* learn to look at a class diagram and visualize its most important interactions.

So let's look at how to do this. First, we'll visualize an association in three-dimensions. Then, we'll visualize message-sends within that new dimension. And finally, we'll walk through a series of class diagram and sequence diagram pairs, so you can begin to visualize those interactions for yourself.

Here we go.

Consider an association with a "0..*" marking on one end (Figure 1-11).

Already, the class diagram is asking us to visualize beyond what it explicitly represents. An object on the left side links to some number of objects on the right side. Visually, you can translate it to something like Figure 1-12.

Again, the class diagram is asking us to see beyond what is explicitly represented. The object on the left interacts with the objects on the right,

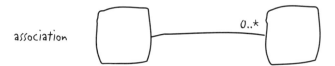

FIGURE 1-11. ▲ An association link.

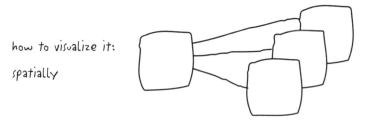

FIGURE 1-12. ▲ How to visualize that link, spatially.

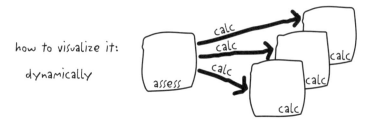

FIGURE 1-13. ▲ How to visualize that link, dynamically.

by sending messages to each one. Figure 1-13 shows how to visualize the implicit dynamics of an association link.

Thankfully, sequence diagrams are explicitly dynamic, giving added visual clues about the sequence of interactions and message sends inherent within a class diagram.

Here are the archetypal interactions for the domain-neutral component—and indeed the archetypal interactions for all components in this book (Figures 1-14 to 1-19).

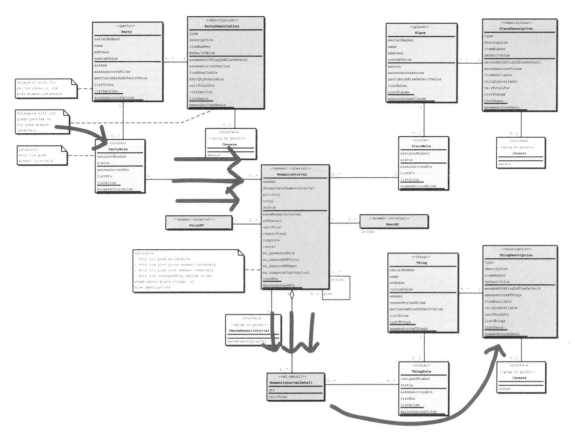

FIGURE 1-14A. ▲ Assess value to business: implicit dynamics.

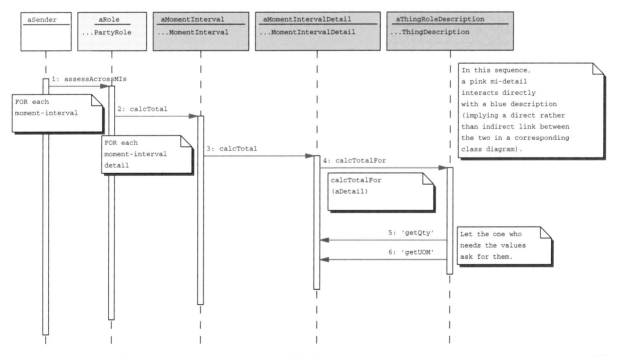

FIGURE 1-14B. ▲ Assess value to business: explicit dynamics.

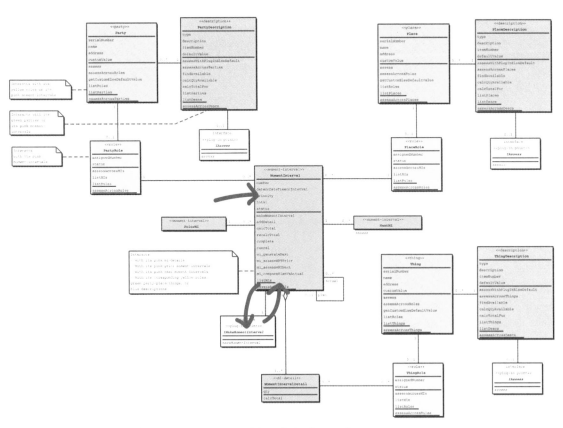

FIGURE 1-15A. ▲ Make moment-interval: implicit dynamics.

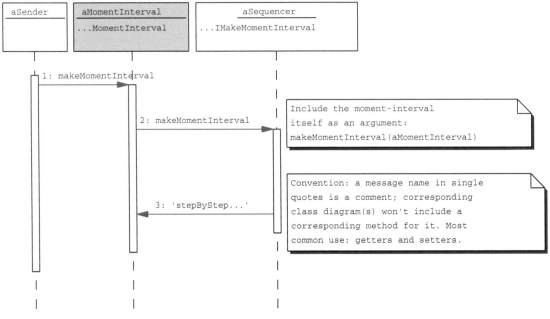

FIGURE 1-15B. ▲ Make moment-interval: explicit dynamics.

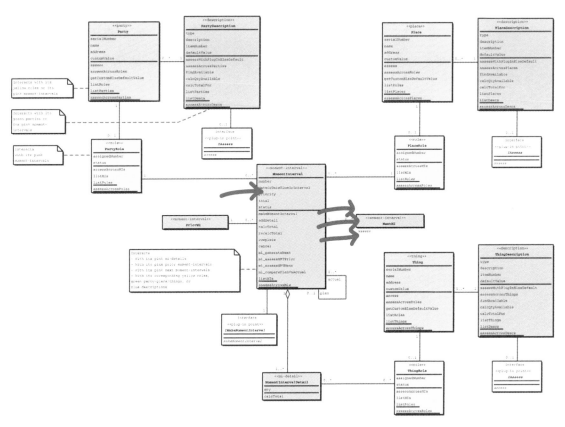

FIGURE 1-16A. ▲ Assess with respect to a subsequent moment-interval: implicit dynamics.

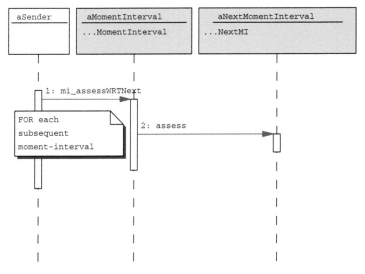

FIGURE 1-16B. ▲ Assess with respect to a subsequent moment-interval: explicit dynamics.

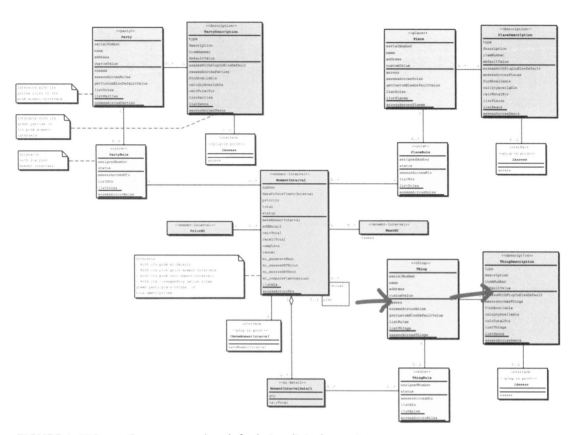

FIGURE 1-17A. ▲ Get custom else default: implicit dynamics.

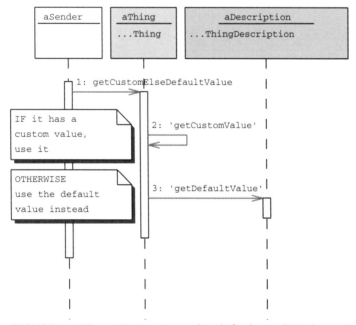

FIGURE 1-17B. ▲ Get custom else default: explicit dynamics.

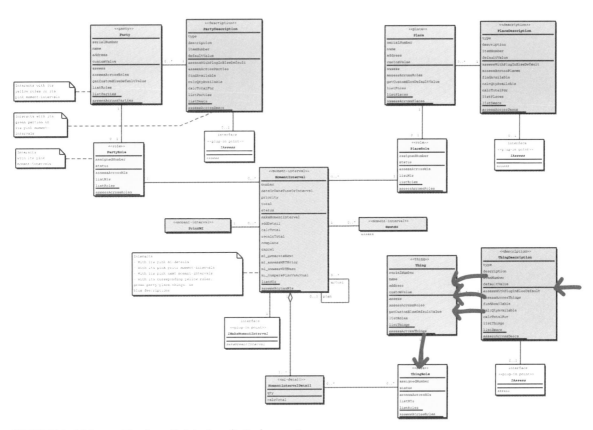

FIGURE 1-18A. ▲ Find available: implicit dynamics.

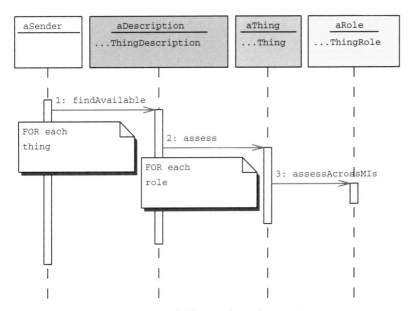

FIGURE 1-18B. ▲ Find available: explicit dynamics.

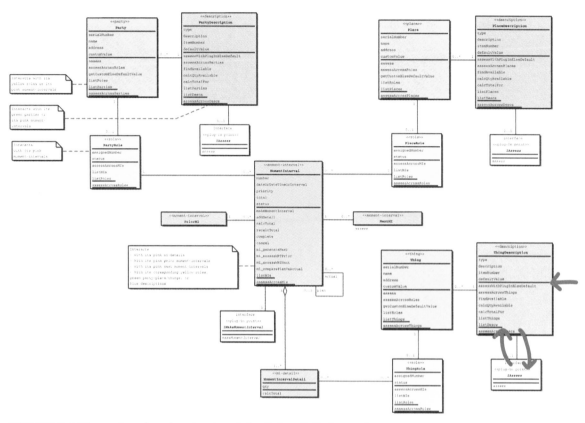

FIGURE 1-19A. ▲ Invoke plug-in else default: implicit dynamics.

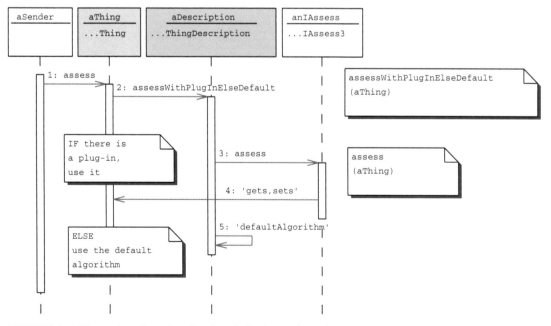

FIGURE 1-19B. ▲ Invoke plug-in else default: explicit dynamics.

1.7 COMPONENT CONNECTIVITY

On printed circuit boards, some components directly connect (that is to say, they are hardwired). Other components plug in. Why not make every element something you can plug in? Sockets everywhere! Well, the reason is that it's simply not cost-effective to do so with printed circuit board design.

The same is true with software components. Some are hardwired, some are plug-in. Although we could have plug-in points everywhere, it's not cost-effective to do so. So we choose and design in plug-in points at those places where we need—and can afford to implement—added flexibility.

The rest of this section moves into a deeper level of detail regarding component connectivity. If you are new to these component concepts, you might wish to skip this for now and come back to it at another time. Yet for those with inquiring minds that want to know, here are the details behind component connectivity.

A "direct connect" links an object in one component with objects in another component (Figure 1-20).

A product-sale object holds a collection of some number of shipments. And a shipment holds a collection of some number of product sales.

We can ask a product sale to assess the timeliness of its shipments; it interacts directly with its shipment objects (Figure 1-21).

And we can ask a shipment if it was shipped before the due dates for its corresponding product sales; it interacts directly with its product-sale objects (Figure 1-22).

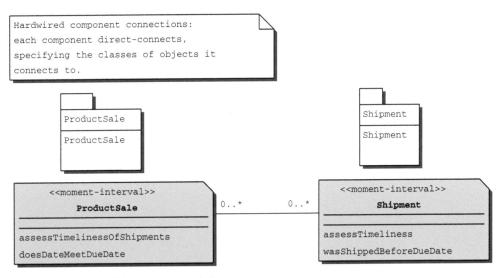

FIGURE 1-20. ▲ Direct connectivity.

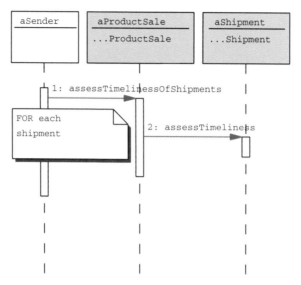

FIGURE 1-21. ▲ Direct connectivity: A product sale interacts with its shipments.

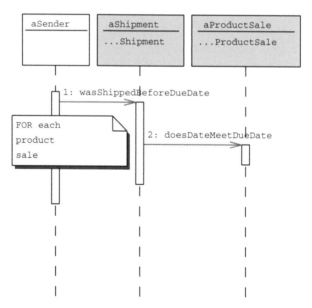

FIGURE 1-22. ▲ Direct connectivity: A shipment interacts with its product sales.

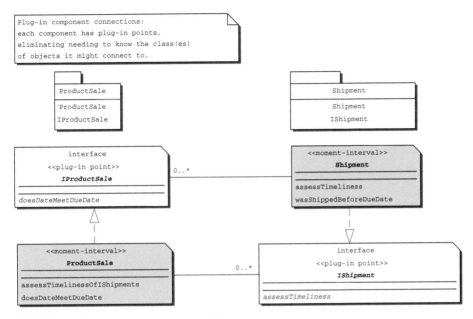

FIGURE 1-23. ▲ Plug-in connectivity.

Now consider plug-in connectivity. An object interacts with whatever is plugged into a plug-in point (Figure 1-23).

A product sale holds a collection of objects from classes that implement the IShipment interface. A shipment holds a collection of objects from classes that implement the IProductSale interface. It really does not matter which classes the connecting objects are in, only that the interface must be implemented.

We can ask a product sale to assess the timeliness of its shipments; it interacts with its IShipment implementers, whatever is plugged into that plug-in point (Figure 1-24).

And we can ask a shipment if it was shipped before the due dates for its corresponding product sales; it interacts with its IProductSale implementers, whatever is plugged into that plug-in point (Figure 1-25).

For modeling simplicity, we build models with direct connections. Then we choose where we want flexibility and add plug-in connectivity (like deciding where we want sockets on a circuit board; it's a decision in adding flexibility).

1.8 TWELVE COMPOUND COMPONENTS

What if you had a substantial collection of enterprise-component models? Each component would establish a fundamental model shape, the most common responsibilities for the classes and interfaces, and the plug-in points for extending capabilities. Each component would give your modeling team something more than a blank whiteboard for getting started in building a model for your application or family of applications.

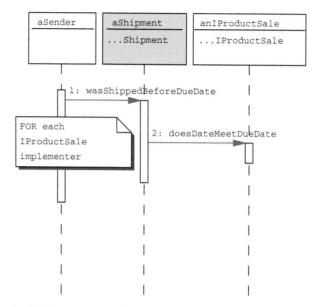

FIGURE 1-24. ▲ Plug-in connectivity: A product sale and its shipments.

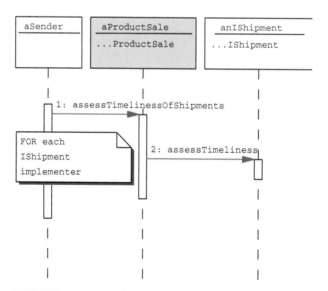

FIGURE 1-25. ▲ Plug-in connectivity: A shipment and its product sales.

This book delivers a collection of 61 enterprise components.

These components are ready to use and reuse as you see fit. You can put them to work in a number of ways, for example:

- Use as-is.
- Extend a component by plugging in new capabilities at the plug-in points.
- Extend by adding additional content.
- Use as a cross-check, an outside opinion, one that you can compare and contrast with your own ongoing work.

The twelve compound components are shown in Figure 1-26.

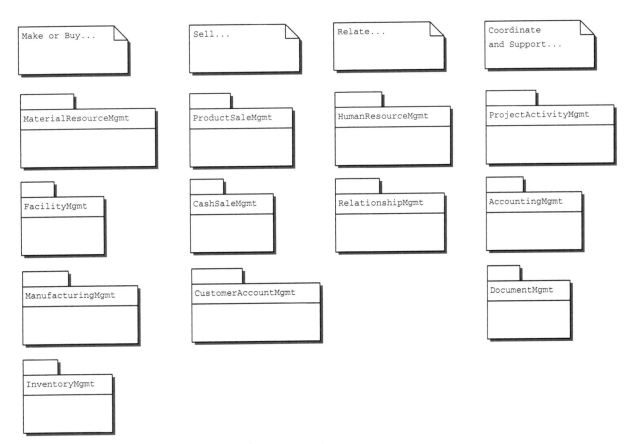

FIGURE 1-26. ▲ The twelve compound components.

1.9 SUGGESTED READING PATHS

You might choose to read this book in any number of ways.

If you are interested in a *sampling of interesting compound components*, read the first major section of each chapter (that is to say, 2.1, 3.1, 4.1, and 5.1).

If you are interested in a *top-down understanding of the components*, begin with project-activity management and then move to its subordinates: material-resource management, facility management, manufacturing management, inventory management, and human-resource management. Then scan the others.

If you are interested in *learning specific modeling tips*, begin by scanning the modeling-tips appendix. Then carefully study Chapter 2. Finally, scan Chapters 3–5 for additional tips. (We present each tip right after we've shown its application by example. Once we present a tip, we do not repeat it in subsequent material. So Chapter 2 has the most tips.)

If you are interested in *the domain-neutral component and its steady application across 61 components*, copy the domain-neutral component with four colors of Post-it Notes and then study the class-diagram shapes in Chapters 2–5, looking at what's the same and what's different, observing the little things along the way.

If you are interested in *templates, plans, and plan executions*, study the sections on manufacturing management and then activity management.

If you are interested in *material resources that eventually become products* and how the two interrelate and interact, read the sections on material-resource management, then product-sale management, and then inventory management.

If you are interested in *system and device interaction*, read the sections on manufacturing management (especially the section on device interaction) and accounting management (the part within accounting payment, dealing with authorization-system interaction).

If you are interested in the *development process*, read Chapter 1, scan Chapters 1–5, and then study Chapter 6.

1.10 SUMMARY

This chapter introduced enterprise-component modeling using color.

In practice, we have developed enterprise-model components and a process for building, applying, and adapting those components. Along the way, we've discovered that encoding added layers of information (roles, moment-intervals, things, and descriptions) was an essential ingredient for both building and reading component models; we found that color was especially suitable for adding these layers of information.

Component modeling with color is so effective that we expect that we will never again return to the monotonous flatland of monochrome modeling.

So get a set of four-color Post-it Notes and try this out for yourself. Take an existing model you are working on—or start with a new one, if you wish. Add "stickers" for the pink moment-intervals; the yellow roles;

the green parties, places, or things; and blue descriptions. Then stand back and check it out. Discuss it with a colleague. Walk through it with a domain expert.

Or, if you already have a large model, get a set of color highlighting pens (pink, yellow, green, and blue) and highlight the class names in your model. This is another good way to get started.

REFERENCES

Color and Visualization

[Chijiiwa87] Chijiiwa, Hideaki, *Color Harmony*. Cincinnati: Rockport Publishers, 1987.

[Gardner83] Gardner, Howard, *Frames of Mind: The Theory of Multiple Intelligences*. New York: Basic Books, 1983.

The Elements of Color. New York: Van Nostrand Reinhold, 1970.

[Root-Bernstein85] Root-Bernstein, Robert Scott, "Visual Thinking: The Art of Imagining Reality." *Transactions of the American Philosophical Society,* Volume 75, 1985.

[Tufte90] Tufte, Edward R., *Envisioning Information*. Cheshire, CT: Graphics Press, 1990.

Walker, Morton, *The Power of Color*. Garden City Park, NY: Avery, 1991.

[Wilcox94] Wilcox, Michael, *Blue and Yellow Don't Make Green,* Revised Edition. Cincinnati: North Light Books, 1994.

Modeling

Booch, Grady, with James Rumbaugh and Ivar Jacobson, *UML User Guide*. Reading, MA: Addison Wesley, 1999.

[Coad97a] Coad, Peter, "Boundary; Colors; Timeline; Status." *The Coad Letter*. Object International (www.oi.com), September 30, 1997.

[Coad97b] Coad, Peter, "How to Build Better Object Models." Tutorial. *OOPSLA*, Atlanta, October 1997.

[Coad92] Coad, Peter, and Mayfield, Mark, "Object-Oriented Patterns." *Communications of the ACM*. September 1992.

[Coad95-97] Coad, Peter with Mark Mayfield and David North, *Object Models: Strategies, Patterns, and Applications*. Second Edition. Upper Saddle River, NJ: Prentice Hall, 1997.

Curran, Thomas, and Gerhard Keller with Andrew Ladd, *SAP R/3 Business Blueprint*. Upper Saddle River, NJ: Prentice Hall, 1998.

Fowler, Martin, *Analysis Patterns*. Reading, MA: Addison Wesley, 1996.

Fowler, Martin, with Kendall Scott, *UML Distilled*. Reading, MA: Addison Wesley, 1997.

Gamma, Erich, Richard Helm, Ralph Johnson, and John Vlissides, *Design Patterns*. Reading, MA: Addison Wesley, 1995.

[Hayakawa68] Hayakawa, S.I., Editor, *Use the Right Word*. Now published under the title *Choose the Right Word*. Pleasantville, NY: Reader's Digest, 1968.

[Webster78] *Webster's New Twentieth Century Dictionary*. New York: Collins World, 1978.

2 Make or Buy

▶ **Example is always more efficacious than precept.**

Samuel Johnson

Chapters 2–5 present the 61 domain-neutral components. Within the chapters, you'll find major sections, each of which contains:

- A *compound component* (for example, material-resource management), plus
- A number of *components* (for example, material-resource, material request, and request-for-quote to supplier)

For each *compound component*, you'll find sections on what it is, its scope, its steps, its links to other compound components, its "mirror image" relationship (if any) with other compound components, its components, its pink moment-intervals, example interactions (an intercomponent sequence diagram), and how it could be further expanded.

For each *component*, you'll find a guided tour of the class-diagram for the component, key methods, example interactions (an intracomponent sequence diagram)—and modeling tips at various points along the way (right at the point you can apply them with success).

This chapter presents four compound components:

1. Material-resource management
2. Facility management
3. Manufacturing management
4. Inventory management

2.1 MATERIAL-RESOURCE MANAGEMENT

What. Material resources are the things that a business uses to get things done. They include the raw materials needed for manufacturing a product. They also include the day-to-day supplies one needs to run a business.

Scope. Material-resource management begins with a request and ends with the fulfillment of that request, including delivery and the processing of an invoice from the supplier.

Steps. First, define material types and materials. Second, request materials, possibly indicating a preferred provider. Third, send a request for quotation (RFQ) to suppliers. Fourth, enter the RFQ answers you receive from those suppliers who choose to respond. Fifth, select a winning answer and issue a corresponding purchase order (PO). Sixth, receive delivery from the supplier. Seventh, enter an invoice from a supplier and post the amount (to the accounting component). Eighth, request and track service from the supplier.

Links. Track the material resources we keep in storage units (inventory management). Post costs (accounting management). Accept requests (from manufacturing, facility, and project-activity management).

Mirror images. In material-resource management, we move things into the business on an invoicing basis (from a supplier to us). In product-sale management, we move things out of the business on an invoicing basis (from us to a customer).

Components. The components within material-resource management are (Figure 2-1):

- Material resource
- Materials request
- RFQ

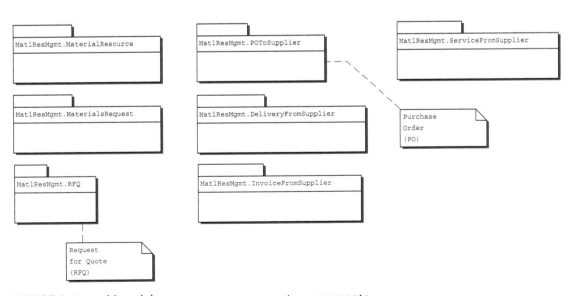

FIGURE 2-1. ▲ Material-resource management components.

- PO to supplier
- Delivery from supplier
- Invoice from supplier
- Service from supplier

Moment-intervals.   The main moment-intervals for material-resource management are (Figure 2-2):

- Materials request
- RFQ
- RFQ answer
- PO to supplier
- Delivery from supplier
- Invoice from supplier
- Service request
- Service from supplier

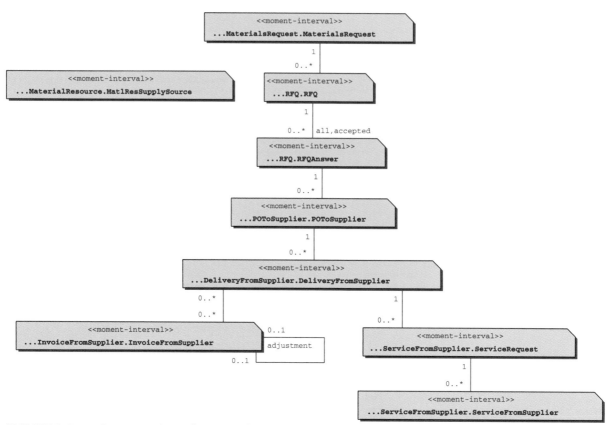

FIGURE 2-2. ▲ Summary in pink: material-resource management.

Interactions. The components work together to get things done. An example of inter-component interaction, "assess request to delivery" (meaning, assess the satisfaction of a request all the way through to delivery), is shown in Figure 2-3. A sender asks a pink materials request to assess its degree of fulfillment. The request traverses from request to pink RFQ, to pink RFQ answer, to pink PO, to one or more pink deliveries. At the end, the request returns the result to the sender.

Expansion. One could expand this compound component by enhancing supplier selection, managing consignment stocks, and establishing supply chains.

2.1.1 Material Resource

Guided tour. The material-resource component is shown in Figure 2-4. The material-resource component has two central classes: a green material resource, and a blue material-resource description.

Material resource. A green material resource is something that a business uses (for example, a specific part or a batch), is individually identifiable (it has a serial or lot number of some kind), and is one that you find you must individually track.

If a material resource were not individually identifiable (for example, one thousand tons of hops), you would not need a green thing; instead, you could use a quantity (one thousand tons) of a blue catalog-entry-like description (hops). Moreover, if something were individually identifiable yet you needed only to track quantities (and not ever answer the question "which one?"), then again a quantity of a blue catalog-entry-like description would be sufficient.

Here's another example. A material resource (green thing) could represent a specific hard-drive subassembly, identifiable by its serial number. A material-resource description object (blue description) could represent a standard catalog entry that applies to any hard-drive subassembly: the manufacturer is Acme, the model number is 1720, and the storage size is 10 gigabytes.

Tip. Green or blue? Use green party/place/thing when it's uniquely identifiable and you need to track it that way. Otherwise, use some quantity of a blue description instead.

A green product links to yellow roles, specific contexts of participating within the model. Those two roles are "a material resource being ordered" and "a material resource being used."

Material-resource description. This is a catalog-entry-like description of a kind of material resource. A blue material-resource description is the main description; it links to a number of other supporting blue context-specific supplemental descriptions that one can add on as needed.

Other components use certain quantities of a material-resource description. For example, if someone requests 15 Acme GT3 laptops, then a component might include a request detail with a quantity of 15, linked

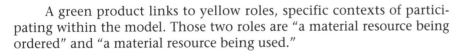

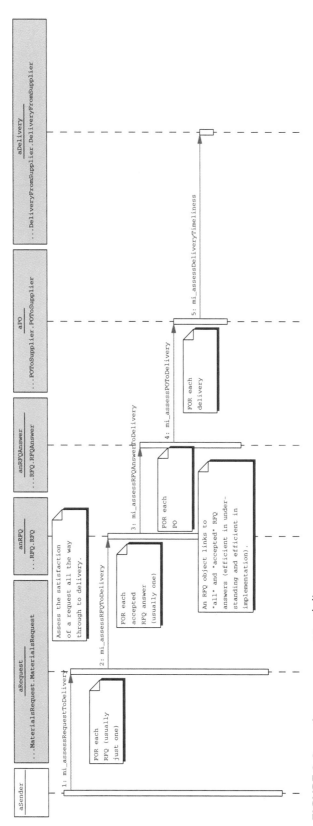

FIGURE 2-3. ▲ Assess request to delivery.

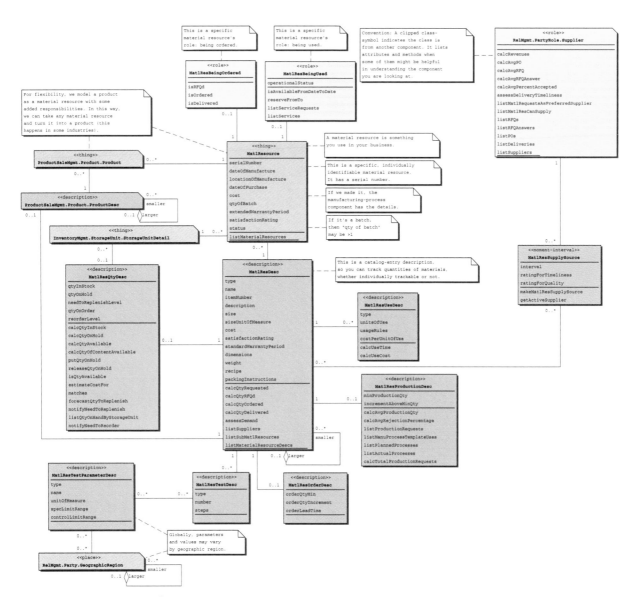

FIGURE 2-4. ▲ Material-resource component.

to a blue material-resource description (more specifically, GT3 laptop description) that applies to each Acme GT3 laptop.

Supply source. A pink supply source maps suppliers and material resources, indicating the interval of time, along with the timeliness and quality ratings for that supplier supplying those material resources.

Methods. Key methods include: calculate quantities requested, quoted, ordered, and delivered; list the suppliers of a material resource; and list the material resources available from a supplier.

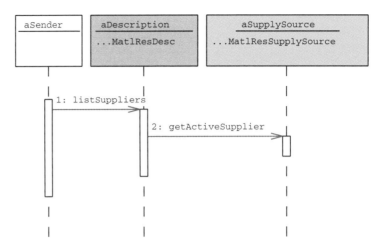

FIGURE 2-5. ▲ List suppliers of a material resource.

Interactions. The "list suppliers of a material resource" sequence is shown in Figure 2-5. A sender asks a blue material-resource description for a list of suppliers. The description asks each of its pink material-resource supply sources[1] to get its active supplier; it checks its status and interval; if okay, it returns its yellow supplier object back to the sender; otherwise it returns a null value back to the sender. At the end, the material-resource description returns a list to the sender.

A pink moment-interval has an interval, some date(s), or some date-time stamp(s). So it's fair game to ask it questions like "Are you applicable on this date I'm giving you?" In addition to applicable interval, a moment-interval knows how to respond to a request for a calculation or some other result.

So a sender could make this a two-step process: first, are you valid for this request; second, please fulfill a request.

Yet that makes the sender know more about the receiver than it needs to. The sender had to know to ask about validity before asking for what it really needed.

It's better to let the sender ask for what it needs: fulfill this request. The sender knows less and interacts less with the receiver. The receiver checks its own validity, returning a null value, returning a zero, or raising an exception when it cannot honor that request (if an exception, the sender must handle it).

 Tip. Validate then do? Merge into a single step for the sender, passing arguments and letting the receiver encapsulate all steps in the process. The receiver validates, performs the requested action, and returns the result to the sender.

---

[1]Material resource supply source (assignment) is pink, why? It's pink because it's an assignment over some interval of time between a yellow supplier role and some number of blue material-resource descriptions.

Also note that what the sender gets back is a list of suppliers, not a list of supplier names and addresses. If the sender needs that information, it can ask a supplier (which in turn will ask its corresponding green person or organization object) for those values. So return a list of objects. Get values from that list (and then from its members) right at the point you need it (not sooner).

Tip. Values from an object several links away? Ask for the object, then ask it for the values you need. Don't pass the command through several layers of intermediaries, unless that command is useful to the intermediary objects as well.

2.1.2 Materials Request

Guided tour. The materials-request component is shown in Figure 2-6. The materials-request component has one pink moment-interval, a materials request.

Materials request. A materials request may come from a user, from a material-resource description based upon its reorder threshold, or from a project-activity request detail, one that a material-resource request supports.

A pink materials request links to two yellow roles, materials requester and supplier. The supplier might be an internal or external supplier. The supplier might be a preferred supplier; the text tag at the end of the link near supplier is a convenient way to annotate the role that a connecting object plays. This text tag allows you to identify a role or context for that link without needing to add a separate class with the same attributes, links, and methods.

Tip. Yellow role with no added responsibilities? Express that yellow role with a text label rather than with another yellow role.

A pink materials request links to pink materials-request detail(s).

Materials-request detail. A pink materials-request detail specifies a quantity of a blue material-resource description (actually a subset of the overall description, relating to quantities). Or it might link to yellow material-resource-being-ordered(s), which in turn links to a green material resource (in the material-resource component).

Note that the link between materials request and materials-request detail is an aggregation, showing the whole and its parts, a bit of added meaning.

Tip. Association or aggregation? Association is by far the norm, the 90 percent case. Use aggregation only when you want to give the added meaning of whole-part, container-content, or group-member.

Before and after. For a materials request, the preceding pink moment-interval is project-activity request detail (in project-activity management). The subsequent pink moment-interval is RFQ.

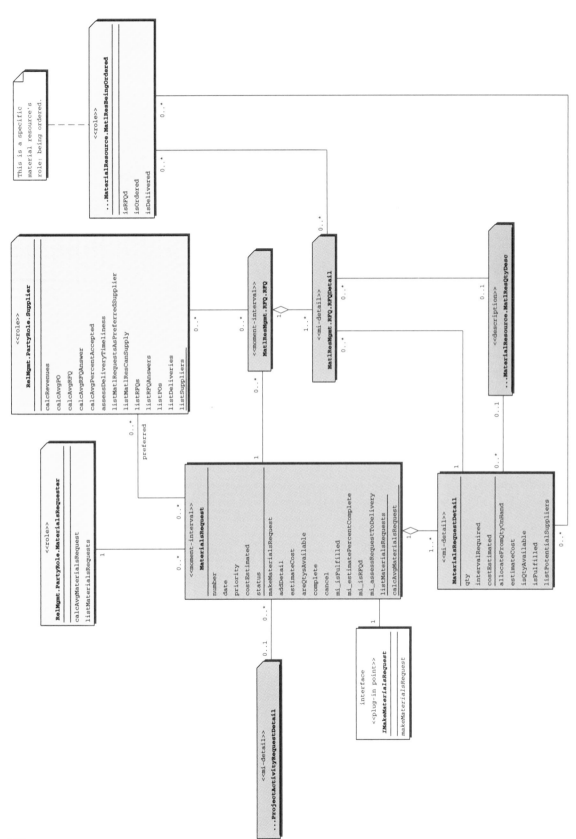

FIGURE 2-6. ▲ Materials-request component.

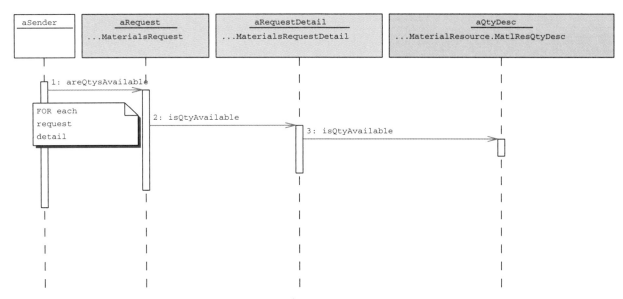

FIGURE 2-7. ▲ Are quantities available to satisfy a request?

Methods. Key methods include: make a materials request, estimate cost, check available quantities, list materials requests for a requester, and list materials request for a supplier when that supplier is designated as a preferred supplier.

Interactions. The "is quantity available" sequence is shown in Figure 2-7. A sender asks a pink request if a quantity is available. That pink request asks each of its pink details if quantities are available. Each pink detail asks its blue material-resource quantity description if quantities are available. A blue description answers the question, returning the appropriate result. At the end, the request returns the result to the sender.

2.1.3 RFQ

Guided tour. The RFQ component is shown in Figure 2-8. The RFQ component has two pink moment-intervals, linked together: RFQ and RFQ answer.

RFQ. A pink RFQ links to a yellow supplier. It also links to pink RFQ detail.

RFQ detail. A pink RFQ detail specifies a quantity of a blue material resource description and the anticipated unit price. Or it might link to one or more yellow "material-resource-being-ordered" roles, each of which links to a green material (in the material-resource component).

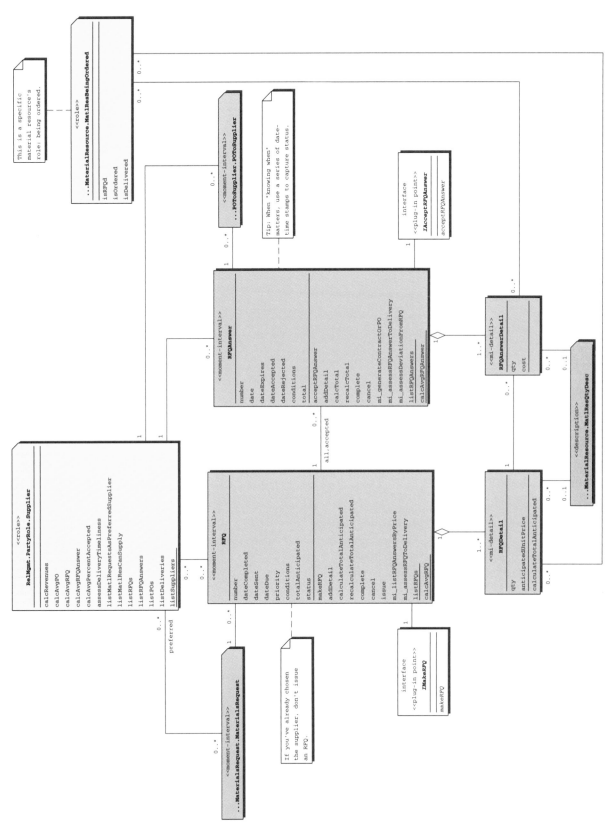

FIGURE 2-8. ▲ RFQ component.

RFQ answer.   A pink RFQ answer links to a yellow supplier (representing an answer and the supplier who sent it in). It also links to the pink RFQ it answers.

RFQ-answer detail.   A pink RFQ-answer detail specifies a quantity of a blue material resource description and a price. Or it might link to one or more yellow "material-resource-being-ordered" roles, each of which links to a green material (in the material-resource component).

Look at the link between a pink RFQ and a pink RFQ answer. An RFQ holds two collections of RFQ answers. One collection includes all of the answers. The other includes only the accepted RFQ answer.

Tip.   Notable subsets? If you want to show that an association or aggregation link has notable subsets, use a qualifier label and list what those subsets are. For example: "all, accepted." Implement a separate member for each collection you list.

Tip.   Repeatedly asking for state? If you find an object repeatedly asking objects it links to what state they are in, let the object hold state-specific collections. That simplifies the design and reduces message traffic.

Before and after.   For RFQ, the preceding pink moment-interval is materials request. For RFQ answer, the subsequent pink moment-interval is PO.

Methods.   Key methods include: make RFQ, accept RFQ answer[2], calculate the anticipated total of an RFQ, list RFQ answers by price, list RFQs sent to a supplier, list RFQ answers received from a supplier, and calculate the average RFQ answer from a supplier.

Interactions.   Suppose you'd like to add a method to calculate the anticipated total for an RFQ. Where would you put the initiating method for that sequence?

Tip.   Where to put a method? Take a feature statement, <action> the <result> <by | for | of | to> a <moment-interval | role | description | party, place, thing>. Put the initiating method in the corresponding class.

Here, we want to "calculate the anticipated total of an RFQ." So we put the initiating method in the RFQ class.

The "calculate total anticipated" sequence is shown in Figure 2-9. A sender asks a pink RFQ to calculate its anticipated total. The RFQ object asks each of its pink RFQ details to do the same: calculate its anticipated total. At that point, each RFQ detail does its work, using its quantity and anticipated unit price. If no anticipated unit price is found, then it gets the list price from the corresponding blue material-resource description or from yellow material-resource being ordered(s). At the end, the RFQ returns the total to the sender.

---

[2]For consistency, we could use the verb "make" here, but that really does not make a lot of sense in this context. So we use "accept" instead.

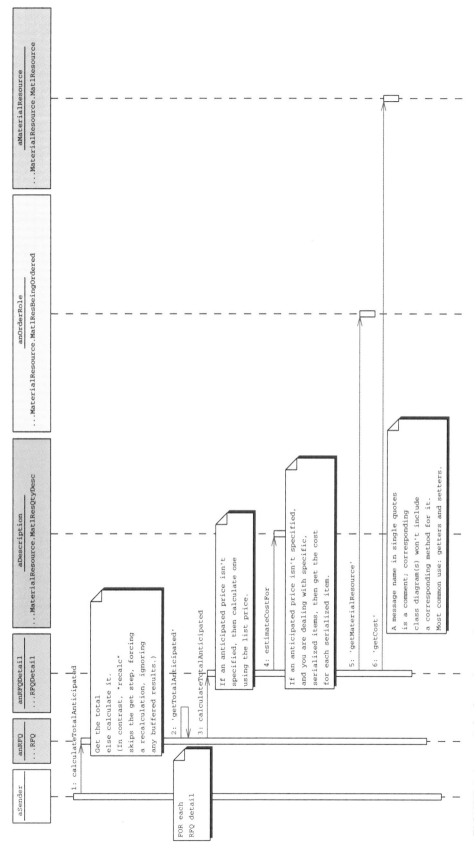

FIGURE 2-9. ▲ Calculate the total you anticipate as a response to an RFQ.

Note that when we ask an RFQ to calculate, the first thing it does is retrieve its buffered amount, saved from a previous calculation. If it does not have a buffered result, it invokes "recalculate," which forces a calculation to occur without regard for whatever might or might not be buffered.

Tip. Calculate and recalculate? Begin with a calculate method. Add a buffered result attribute if values or plug-in algorithms might change on you, affecting the result of the calculation. Add a recalculate method if you need a way to force recalculation (ignoring any buffered value).

2.1.4 PO to Supplier

Guided tour. The PO-to-supplier component is shown in Figure 2-10. The purchase-order-to-supplier component has one pink moment-interval, PO to supplier.

PO to supplier. A pink PO to supplier links to three yellow roles: buyer, supplier, and point-of-contact (the point-of-contact for this particular PO). It also links to pink PO detail(s).

PO detail. A PO detail specifies a quantity of a material resource (just part of the material-resource description is included here, called a material resource quantity description). Or it might link to yellow material-resources order role(s), which in turn link to a green material (in the material-resource component).

Before and after. For PO to supplier, the preceding pink moment-intervals are RFQ answer and project-activity detail (in project-activity management). The subsequent pink moment-interval is delivery.

Methods. Key methods include: make purchase order, calculate total, calculate total discount, assess a buyer's effectiveness at getting discounts, assess deviation from RFQ answer, and list items purchased but not yet delivered.

Interactions. The "assess a buyer's effectiveness at getting discounts" sequence is shown in Figure 2-11. We ask a yellow buyer how effective it is at getting discounts. That yellow role holds a collection of pink moment intervals, POs, all with discounts. So the role interacts with its POs, asking each one to calculate its total discount. And each PO interacts with its details, asking each one to calculate its total discount. At the end, the buyer returns the assessment result to the sender.

Note that when we ask a PO to calculate, the first thing it does is retrieve its buffered total, saved from a previous calculation. If it does not have a buffered result, it invokes "recalculate," which forces a calculation to occur without regard for whatever might or might not be buffered. The same is true when we ask a PO detail to calculate its total.

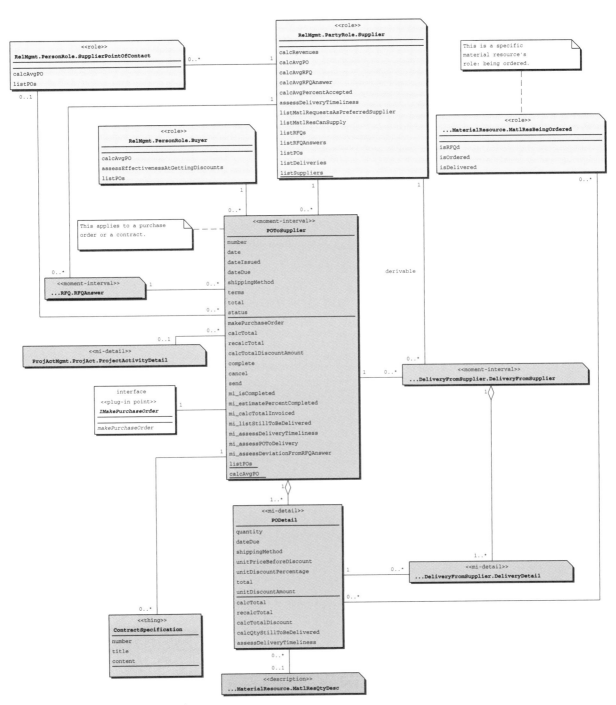

FIGURE 2-10. ▲ PO-to-supplier component.

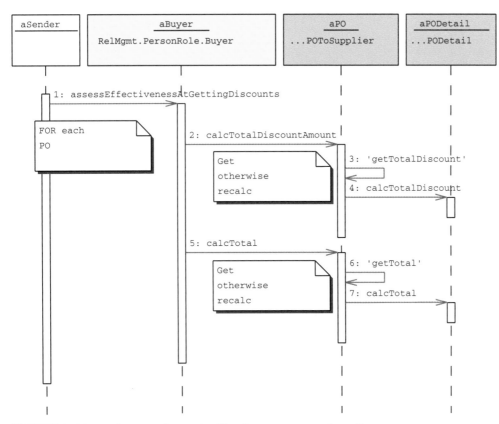

FIGURE 2-11. ▲ Assess a buyer's effectiveness at getting discounts.

2.1.5 Delivery from Supplier

Guided tour. The delivery component is shown in Figure 2-12. The delivery-from-supplier component has one pink moment-interval, delivery from supplier.

Delivery from supplier. A pink delivery from supplier links to one yellow role, supplier. It also links to pink delivery detail(s).

Delivery detail. A pink delivery detail specifies quantity received, accepted, and rejected. A delivery detail links back to a pink PO detail for purchasing specifics. It also links to green storage-unit details, recording where those delivered items go once we receive them (for example, one 50-pound sack of malt, going into this storage unit: bin A27B-00-37 on shelf 10-1 in aisle 10 in warehouse 5).

Before and after. For delivery, the preceding pink moment-interval is PO. The subsequent pink moment-intervals are invoice from supplier and service request.

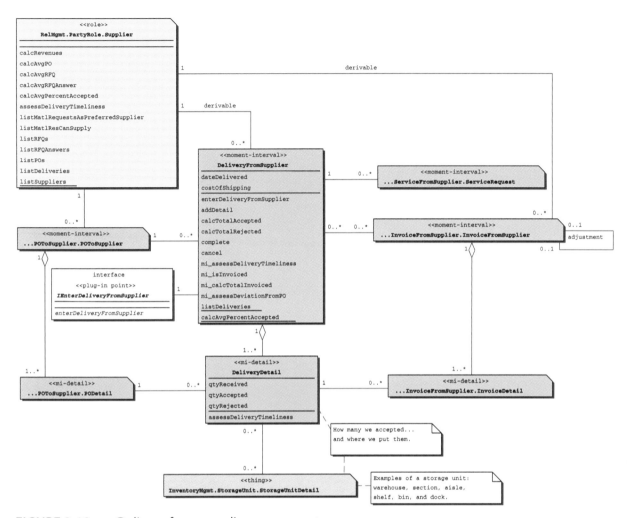

FIGURE 2-12. ▲ Delivery-from-supplier component.

Methods. Key methods include: enter delivery, assess deviation, and assess delivery timeliness by a supplier.

Interactions. The "assess delivery timeliness" sequence is shown in Figure 2-13. A sender asks a pink delivery to assess its timeliness. That delivery interacts with its pink delivery details, asking each one to assess its timeliness. Finally, each delivery detail interacts with its corresponding pink PO detail, which knows a corresponding due date and can assess delivery timeliness. At the end, the delivery returns the assessment result to the sender.

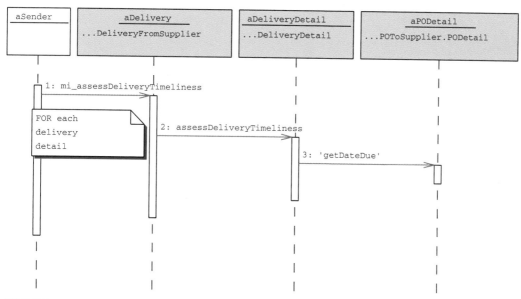

FIGURE 2-13. ▲ Assess timeliness of deliveries from a supplier.

2.1.6 Invoice from Supplier

Guided tour. The invoice component is shown in Figure 2-14. The invoice-from-supplier component has one pink moment-interval, invoice from supplier.

Invoice from supplier. A pink invoice from supplier links to two yellow roles, supplier and accountant. It also links to pink invoice detail(s).

Invoice detail. A pink invoice detail links back to a pink delivery detail and then back to a PO detail, to get purchase specifics. It also links to some yellow material-resource order roles.

Before and after. For invoice, the preceding pink moment-interval is delivery. The subsequent pink moment-interval is an accounting posting of the invoice amount.

Methods. Key methods include: enter invoice from supplier, check if invoices exceed the corresponding PO, check to see if an accountant is authorized to post an amount on a given date, and post the invoice to the business financial records.

Interactions. The "will PO be exceeded" sequence is shown in Figure 2-15a. A sender asks a pink invoice to check to see if its amount will cause the PO amount to be exceeded. A pink invoice sends a message to pink delivery, then a delivery to a pink PO, to ask a PO to calculate the total amount invoiced. Then a PO messages each of its pink deliveries

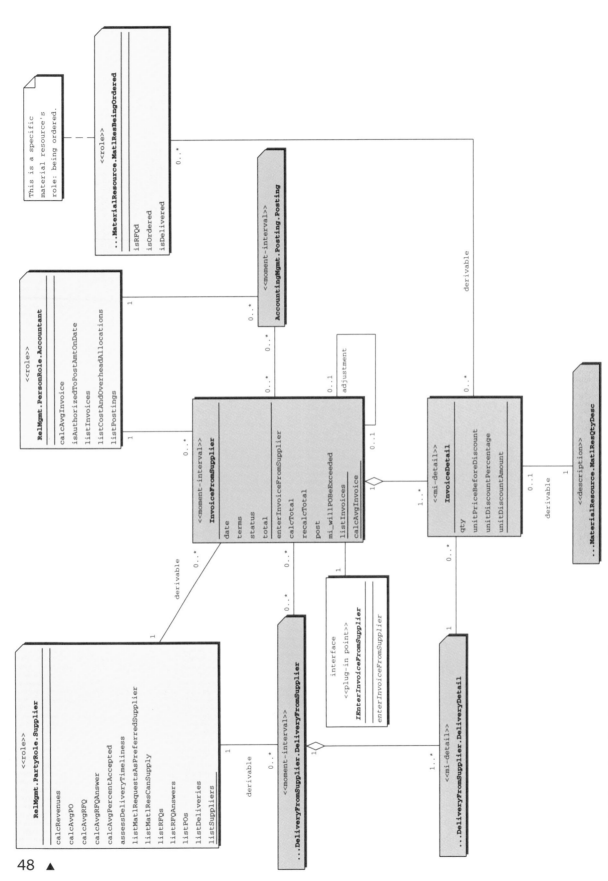

FIGURE 2-14. ▲ Invoice-from-supplier component.

48 ▲

and subsequent invoices, to tally the total invoiced for that PO. The PO returns its result. And the invoice returns its answer to the sender.

We can make the sequence simpler by asking for a PO object and then sending a message directly to it. Using this approach, a delivery does not need a method just to forward the request to the PO. See Figure 2-15b.

We can make it even simpler. By adding an extra (redundant) link from pink invoice back to pink PO, we could make a single message-send. This adds an extra step each time we create a new invoice (we have to establish the link). Yet it simplifies the object interactions in the sequence diagram and in implementation. See Figure 2-15c.

Tip. Add extra associations? Add extra associations to simplify frequent object interactions that would otherwise traverse across a number of intermediary objects (simpler design, simpler implementation).

2.1.7 Service from Supplier

Guided tour. The service component is shown in Figure 2-16. The service-from-supplier component has a pair of pink moment-intervals, linked together: service request and service from supplier.

Service request. A pink service request links to two yellow roles, service requester and service rep. It might link to yellow material-resource-being-used(s), which in turn link to a green material (in the material-resource component). A pink service request links to pink service(s) from supplier(s).

Service from supplier. A pink service-from-supplier links to a yellow service rep.

Before and after. For service request, the preceding pink moment-interval is delivery. For service from supplier, the subsequent pink moment-intervals are accounting posting and perhaps a "service-from-supplier"–related invoice detail.

Methods. Key methods include: enter service request, enter service from supplier, evaluate the closure rate (requests satisfied per some unit of time) for a requester, and evaluate the closure rate of a service rep.

Note that both a requester and a service rep can calculate a closure rate. Should you factor out this common functionality? The key issue is how big is the method. If it is just a few lines of code, then put it in both places; the method will be easier to find, easier to work with, and easier to maintain. If it is something larger, you have three choices: *One,* put the method in both places. *Two,* use inheritance. If both classes can be generalized into a domain-based generalization, you can put the common functionality there. In Java and in good practice, you are limited to just one inheritance link; you may find that you need to use inheritance to satisfy other needs. *Three,* add algorithm plug-in points and then plug-in the functionality each time you create an object in either class; this is the most flexible yet also requires more infrastructure to accomplish.

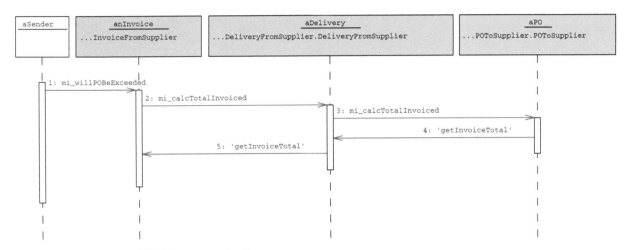

FIGURE 2-15A. ▲ Will PO be exceeded?

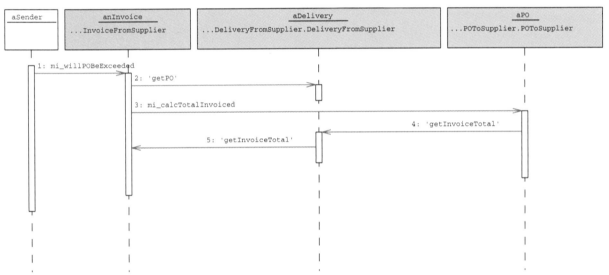

FIGURE 2-15B. ▲ Will PO be exceeded? (simpler)

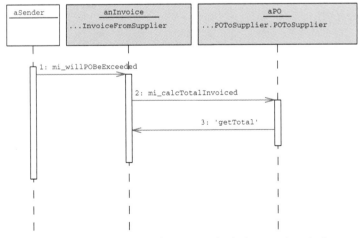

FIGURE 2-15C. ▲ Will PO be exceeded? (even simpler)

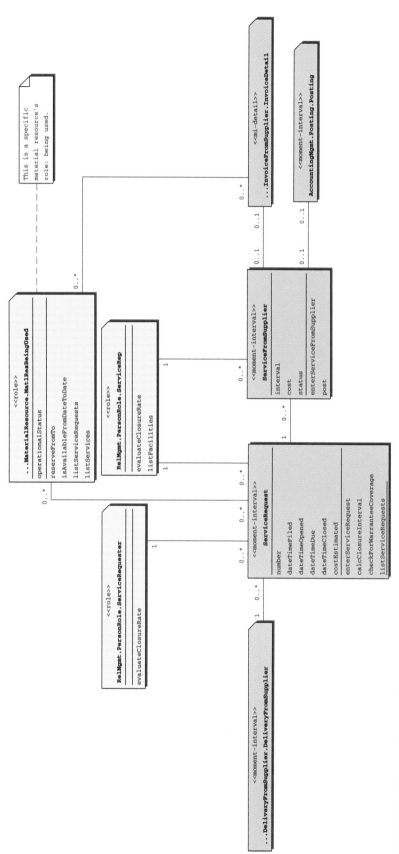

FIGURE 2-16. ▲ Service-from-supplier component.

▲ 51

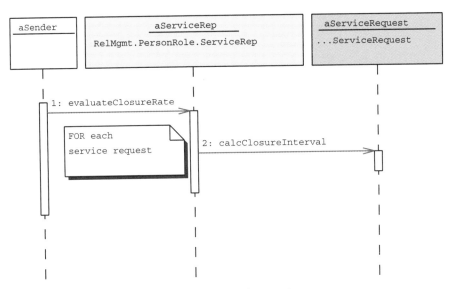

FIGURE 2-17. ▲ Evaluate closure rate of a service rep.

Tip. Common functionality? If small, don't factor it out. If larger, consider using domain-based inheritance or algorithm plug-in points.

Interactions. The "evaluate closure rate for a service rep" sequence is shown in Figure 2-17. A sender asks a yellow service rep object to determine its closure rate. The service rep object asks each of its pink service requests, asking for its closure interval (the amount of time between the date-time opened and the date-time closed). At the end, the service rep returns the closure rate to the sender.

2.2 FACILITY MANAGEMENT

What. Facilities are the building units (buildings and rooms inside), equipment, and vehicles that a business uses to accomplish its business objectives. Facilities are the fixed assets of a business.

Examples. Some examples of facilities under facility management are:

- Networks at a telecommunications company
- Power grids at an electric company
- Cars at a car-rental company
- Branch buildings at a bank
- Stores at a retail company
- Blast furnace at a steel mill
- Stock control point for an assembly line

Scope.   Facility management begins with facility acquisition and ends with maintenance.

Steps.   First, define facility types and facilities. Second, get a budget. Third, plan facility development. Fourth, plan facility-development tasks. Fifth, establish construction contracts for upcoming or currently active tasks. Sixth, work with users to reserve and use facilities. Seventh, based upon inputs from users and inspections, establish problem reports, generate work orders, and conduct maintenance.

Links.   Use in a manufacturing process step (manufacturing management). Move materials and products into and out of a facility's storage locations (inventory management). Plan and control the maintenance activities (project-activity management). Adhere to the budget (accounting management).

Components.   The components within facility management are (Figure 2-18):

- Facility description
- Facility
- Facility development
- Facility-development task
- Facility use
- Facility maintenance

Moment-intervals.   The main moment-intervals for facility management are (Figure 2-19):

- Facility-development request
- Facility development
- Facility-development task
- Construction contract
- Construction-contract charge
- Facility inspection

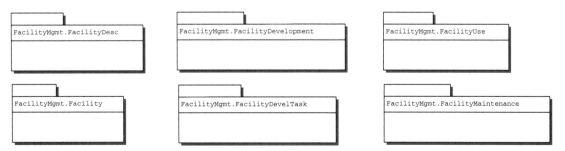

FIGURE 2-18. ▲ Facility-management components.

- Facility-use request
- Facility use (and detail)
- Facility problem
- Facility maintenance request
- Facility maintenance

Interactions.   The components work together to get things done. An example of inter-component interaction, "assess problem resolution from inspection to maintenance," is shown in Figure 2-20. A sender asks a facility development object to assess its problem resolutions. The request traverses from development to inspection to problem to work order to maintenance. At the end, the facility development returns the assessment to the sender.

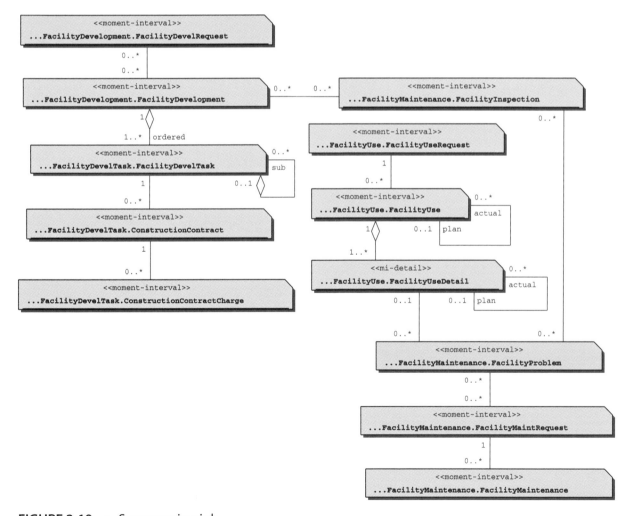

FIGURE 2-19. ▲ Summary in pink.

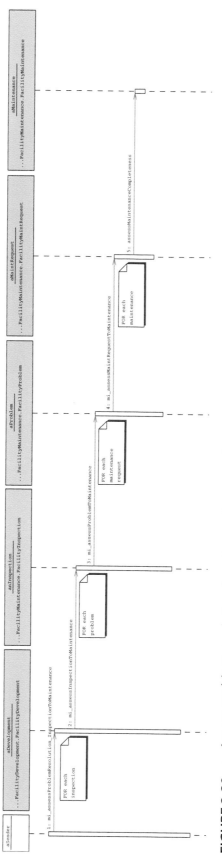

FIGURE 2-20. ▲ Assess problem resolution from inspection to maintenance.

Expansion. One could expand this compound component by adding content to facilities (expanding the kinds of facilities and components within a facility) and by adding the maintenance of those facilities.

2.2.1 Facility Description and Facility

Guided tour. The facility-description and facility components are shown in Figures 2-21a and 2-21b. The facility and facility description components are a closely related pair. They work together to establish and maintain information about kinds of facilities and the operating status of specific facilities participating in specific ways in the business.

Facility description. The blue facility-description class specializes into vehicle description, equipment description, and building-unit description. A blue facility description may link to some number of green facilities.

Note that in Figures 2-21a and 2-21b, the "facility" and "facility description" class names are italicized. This indicates those classes are abstract, meaning they have no corresponding objects. To use them, you must add specialization classes (for example, facility specializing into vehicle, equipment, and building) via inheritance.

Facility. The green facility class specializes into a vehicle, piece of equipment, and building unit. A green facility links to four yellow roles: facility in development, facility as business location, facility in use, and facility in maintenance.

Tip. When to use inheritance? Use inheritance to express specialized moment-intervals, descriptions, or party/place/things.

Tip. When not to use inheritance? Not for "is a role played by a" (use a yellow role instead). Not for changes of what you know about something over time (use pink moment-intervals to show that progression). Not to factor out an algorithm (use a plug-in point instead).

Here's another point: Note that equipment description includes a manufacturer attribute. When you find that an attribute or some word within an attribute names some other problem-domain class, consider whether or not to add that class. In this case, it's manufacturer. If within scope, we could model it as a yellow role played by a green organization, with methods like "list vehicle descriptions" and "rank vehicle descriptions by number of units sold."

Tip. Class name hidden as an attribute name or within an attribute name? Move it out to its own class, if the added capability is within your scope.

Methods. Key methods include calculate available capacity (for a facility, for a facility of this type), allocate work to a facility within a facility pool, level facility use within a facility pool, and assess whether to maintain or replace a facility in maintenance.

Interactions. The "calculate the available capacity for facilities of this type" sequence is shown in Figure 2-22. A sender sends a message to a

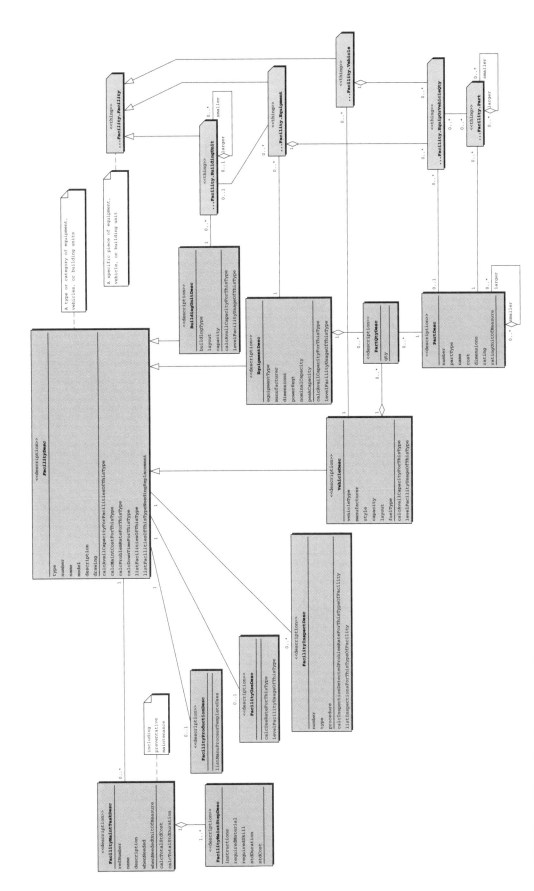

FIGURE 2-21A. ▲ Facility-description component.

▲ 57

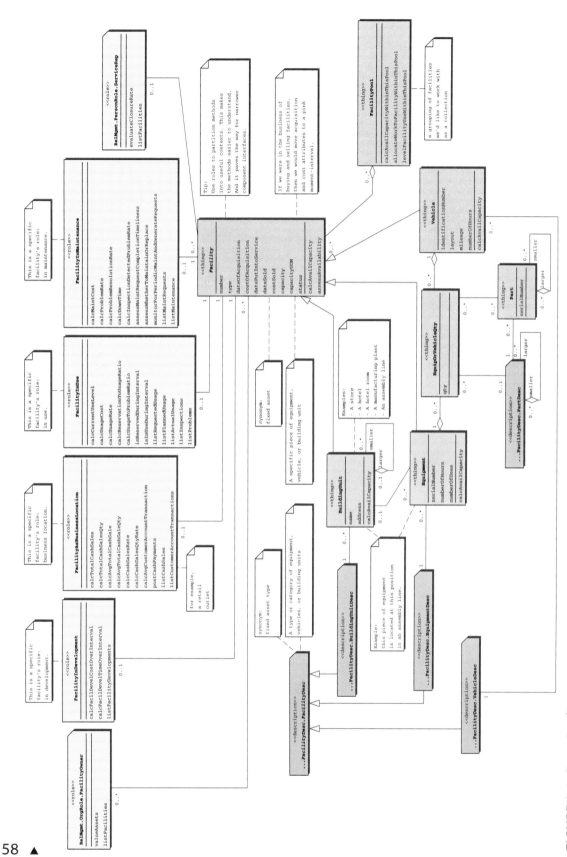

FIGURE 2-21B. ▲ Facility component.

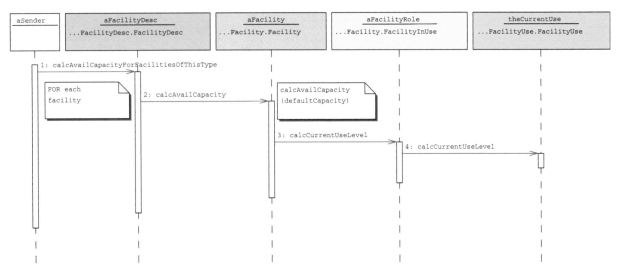

FIGURE 2-22. ▲ Calculate available capacity for facilities of this type.

blue facility description, asking it to calculate the available capacity for that facility type. A facility description then sends a message to each of its green facilities, asking each one to calculate its available capacity (it passes along the default capacity). A facility knows its custom capacity (if it has one) and now the default capacity (passed as an argument). So if it can find out the current use level, it can work out the answer. Each facility asks its corresponding yellow facility-in-use role to calculate its current use level. Finally, the role iterates across its collection of pink facility-use objects (in a component coming up several sections from now), asking it to calculate its current use level. At the end, the facility description returns the available capacity to the sender.

2.2.2 Facility Development

Guided tour. The facility-development component is shown in Figure 2-23. The facility-development component consists of two pink moment-intervals, linked together: facility-development request and facility development.

Facility-development request. A pink facility-development request starts off the sequence. (Note that this request is so simple that we included both request and fulfillment in the same component.) A pink facility-development request links to a yellow facility planner.

Facility development. A pink facility development links to three yellow roles: facility planner, facility developer, and facility-in-development.

Before and after. For a facility-development request, the preceding pink moment-interval is project-activity request detail. For a facility development,

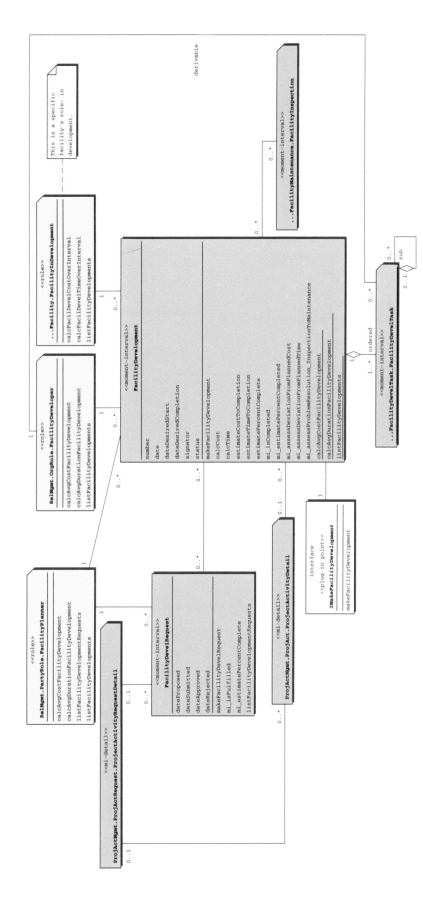

FIGURE 2-23. ▲ Facility-development component.

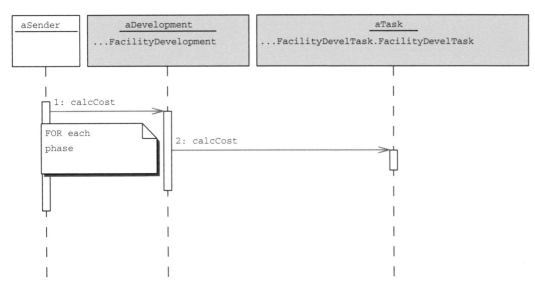

FIGURE 2-24. ▲ Calculate cost (part 1; the next component continues with part 2).

the preceding pink moment-interval is project-activity detail; its subsequent pink moment-intervals are facility-development task and facility inspection.

Methods. Key methods include: make facility development, calculate time and cost, estimate time and cost to completion, and calculate the average duration and cost for a facility development.

Interactions. The "calculate facility development cost (part 1)" sequence is shown in Figure 2-24. A sender asks a pink facility development to calculate cost. A facility development asks each of its pink facility-development tasks to calculate cost. (The next component picks up where this thread leaves off.) At the end, the facility development returns the cost to the sender.

2.2.3 Facility-Development Task

Guided tour. The facility-development-task component is shown in Figure 2-25. The facility-development task component consists of two pink moment-intervals, linked together: facility-development task and construction contract.

Facility-development task. A pink facility-development task links to a yellow facility developer.

Consider that link for a moment. That link is redundant with existing links. In other words, it is *derivable,* meaning that this link is a shortcut to obtaining the needed class at the other end of the association by following the other links. For example, in this case, you can get the link by traversing from facility-development task back to facility development

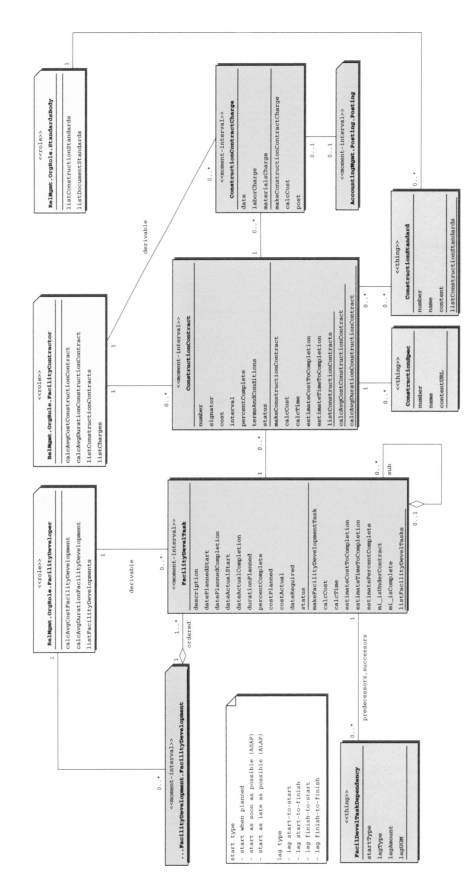

FIGURE 2-25. ▲ Facility-development task component.

(cardinality is 1; the link must be there), and then back to facility developer (cardinality is 1; the link must be there).

Tip. Derivable link? Sometimes you'd like to show a link from class A to class B, even though that link is derivable by following two or more required links from B back to A. This often happens when modeling yellow roles and a sequence of pink moment-intervals. Show the extra link. Label it "derivable" so others know the link is for model expressiveness (not necessarily for implementation).

Now let's continue with the pink facility-development task. It links to green facility-development task dependencies; each dependency object links predecessor and successor dependencies. A facility-development task also links to pink construction contract(s).

Construction contract. A pink construction contract links to a yellow facility contractor. A pink construction contract might have green construction specs and construction standards. A green construction standard links to a yellow standards-body.

Before and after. For a facility-development task, the preceding pink moment-intervals are facility development and budget. For a construction contract, the subsequent pink moment-interval is a pink construction-contract charge followed by a pink accounting posting.

Methods. Key methods include: make facility-development task, calculate time and cost, estimate time and cost to completion, and calculate the average duration and cost for a contractor's contracts. Other key methods would involve changing the planned dates and having that reflected throughout the model.

Interactions. The "calculate cost (part 2)" sequence is shown in Figure 2-26. A sender asks each pink facility-development task to calculate its costs. Each task asks each pink construction contract to calculate its cost; and each construction contract asks each of its pink construction-contract charges to calculate its cost. The task returns the cost to the sender.

2.2.4 Facility Use

Guided tour. The facility-use component is shown in Figure 2-27. The facility-use component consists of two pink moment-intervals, linked together: facility-use request and facility use.

Facility-use request. A pink facility-use request links to two yellow roles: facility user and facility in use. It also links to pink facility use(s).

Facility use. A pink facility use links to a yellow facility user. A facility user links to both current and all of its uses. Also, a pink planned facility use links to subsequent actual facility uses. A facility use links to pink facility-use detail(s).

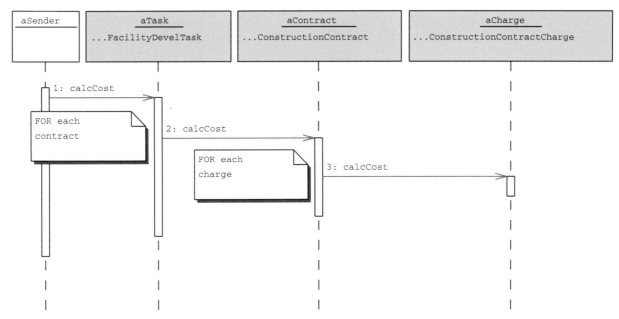

FIGURE 2-26. ▲ Calculate cost (part 2, a continuation from the preceding component shown in Figure 2-24).

Facility-use detail. A facility-use detail links to a blue facility-use description, which links to blue facility description (in the facility component). Or a facility-use detail links to some yellow facility-in-use roles, each of which links to a green facility (in the facility component).

Before and after. For a facility-use request, the preceding pink moment-interval is a project-activity request detail (in project-activity management). For a facility use, the preceding pink moment-interval is a project-activity detail (in project-activity management). For a facility-use detail, its subsequent pink moment-intervals are facility problem and accounting posting.

Methods. Key methods include: make facility use, list planned and actual facility use, assess conversion rate from request to plan, and assess both request-to-plan and request-to-actual ratios.

Interactions. The "assess request-to-actual ratio" sequence is shown in Figure 2-28. A sender asks the pink facility-use request class, the class itself, to assess its request-to-actual ratio.

An interesting point; let's explore this a bit. In the class diagram, in the pink facility-use request class, the "assess request-to-actual ratio" method is underlined. The underlining signifies that this method is a class (static) method, meaning it is defined for the class, rather than for each object in the class.

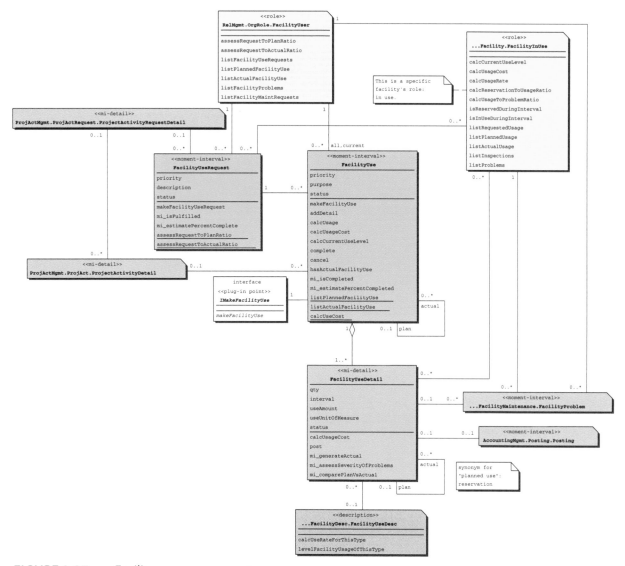

FIGURE 2-27. ▲ Facility-use component.

Tip. Behavior across a collection? Use class methods to express behavior across the collection of all of the objects in a class. Use problem-domain objects to express behavior across the collection of objects it links to. Rarely needed: add another class, a "pool" class, to express behavior across some other collection.

As long as you want to express behavior across the collection of all of the objects in a class, using class methods is much more compact than adding a separate class just to have an object that can hold the collection that you need to work on. In this case, adding both a "facility-use" class and a "collection of all facility uses" class to the model. That would be

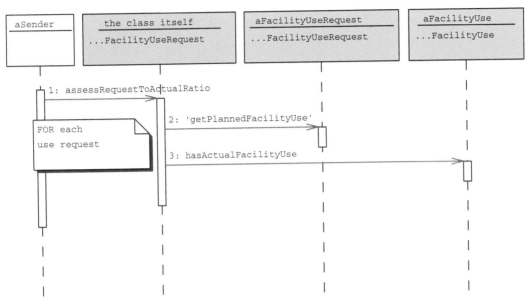

FIGURE 2-28. ▲ Assess facility request-to-actual-use ratio.

very explicit yet would also nearly double the size of your model, while adding very little in terms of model content.

Back to the sequence. The pink facility-use request class asks each of the objects in that class to get its planned facility-use (if it has one); the pink facility-use request class then asks a planned facility-use object if it has an actual plan. At the end, the facility-use request returns the ratio to the sender.

2.2.5 Facility Maintenance

Guided tour. The facility-maintenance component is shown in Figure 2-29. The facility-maintenance component has four key pink moment-intervals, linked together in series. They are inspection, problem, request, and maintenance.

Facility inspection. A pink facility inspection links to a yellow facility-inspector role. It links to a blue facility-inspection description (describing what inspections need to be accomplished). It links to yellow facility-in-use (a role played by a green facility). It also links to pink facility problem(s).

Facility problem. A pink facility problem links to a yellow facility user. It also links to pink facility-maintenance request(s).

Facility-maintenance request. A pink facility maintenance request links to a yellow facility user. It links to some yellow facility-in-maintenance roles, each of which links to a green facility (in the facility component). It also links to pink facility maintenance(s).

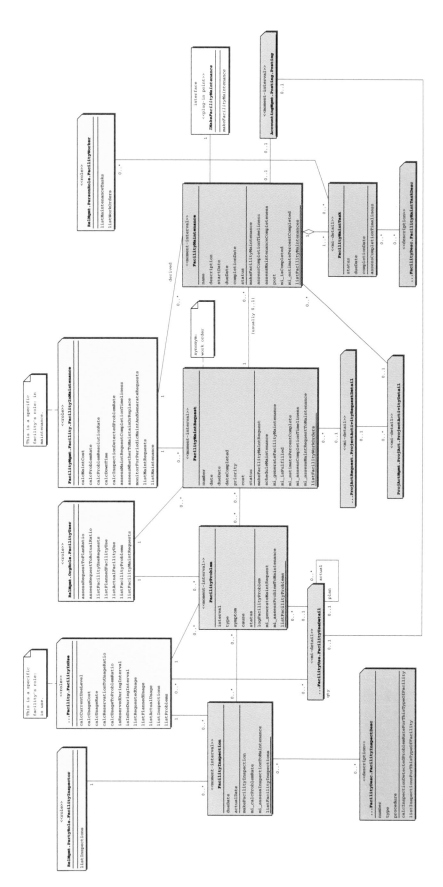

FIGURE 2-29. ▲ Facility-maintenance component.

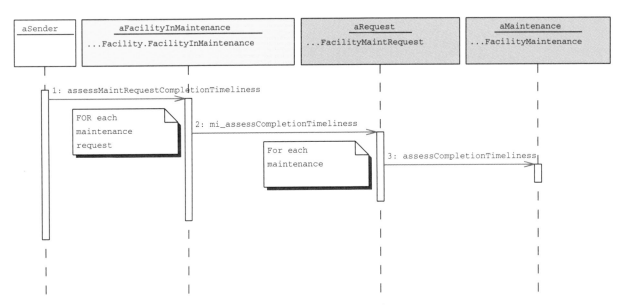

FIGURE 2-30. ▲ Assess maintenance-request completion timeliness.

Facility maintenance. A pink facility maintenance links to pink facility-maintenance task(s). Each facility-maintenance task links to yellow facility worker(s) and to a blue facility-maintenance description (describing the task to be accomplished).

Before and after. For a facility problem, the preceding pink moment-interval is a facility-use detail. For facility maintenance, the subsequent pink moment-interval is an accounting posting of the cost.

Methods. Key methods include: make inspection, log problem, make maintenance request, make maintenance, generate maintenance request, schedule maintenance, and assess completion timeliness for facility maintenance.

Interactions. The "assess maintenance-request completion timeliness" sequence is shown in Figure 2-30. A sender sends a message to a yellow facility-in-maintenance, which then messages its pink facility-maintenance requests. Each facility-maintenance request sends a message to each of its pink facility-maintenance objects, asking each one to assess its completion timeliness. At the end, the facility-in-maintenance returns its assessment to the sender.

2.3 MANUFACTURING MANAGEMENT

What. Manufacturing is the making of goods or articles. Manufacturing management includes establishing production requests, developing process templates, developing process plans, and executing those process plans.

Scope. Manufacturing management begins with requests and ends with actual manufacturing processes, including both building and testing steps.

Steps. First, establish production requests (materials in, materials out, and products out). Second, define templates, plans that have relative times rather than absolute times. Third, with a template and a starting date and time, generate a planned process from a template. Fourth, carry out that process, noting what you actually do along the way, so you can compare your planned process with your actual process (Figures 2-31 and 2-32).

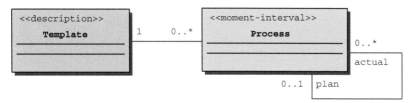

FIGURE 2-31. ▲ From template to planned process to actual process.

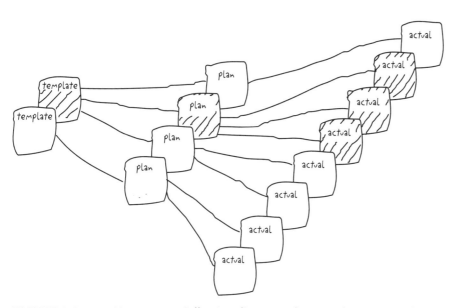

FIGURE 2-32. ▲ How to spatially visualize template to plan to actual process.

Links. Establish a production request in response to one or more sales or in response to a sales forecast (sales management). Use materials from inventory; produce materials and products for inventory (inventory management). Accept project-activity requests (project-activity management). Post manufacturing costs (accounting management).

Components. The components within manufacturing management are (Figure 2-33):

- Production requests
- Process template
- Process
- Supervisory control and data acquisition (SCADA)

Moment-intervals. The main moment-intervals for manufacturing management are (Figure 2-34):

- Production request
- Manufacturing process
- Manufacturing process test result
- Data set
- Number-crunching result
- Pattern-match result

Interactions. The components work together to get things done. An example of inter-component interaction, "assess satisfaction of a request," is shown in Figure 2-35. A sender asks a request to assess the satisfaction of that request. A request object then messages each of its request details. Each request detail asks each of its corresponding actual processes to calculate the quantities it has produced. Each actual process interacts with its

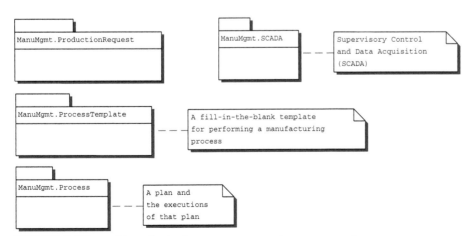

FIGURE 2-33. ▲ Manufacturing-management components.

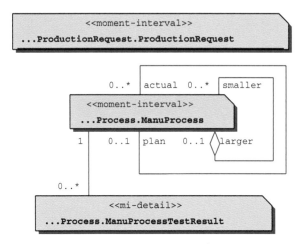
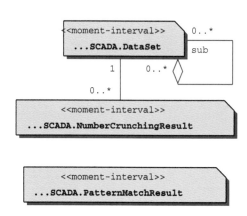

FIGURE 2-34. ▲ Summary in pink.

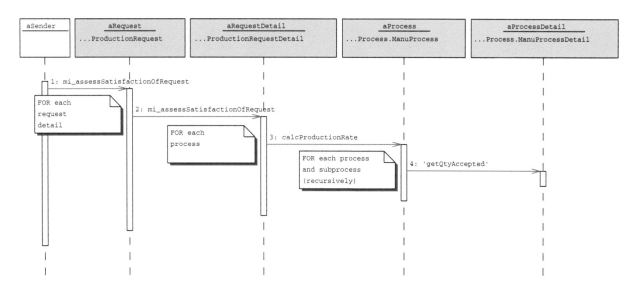

FIGURE 2-35. ▲ Assess satisfaction of a request.

sub-processes. Each process and sub-process interacts with its process details, to work out the answer. At the end, a request returns its assessment to the sender.

Expansion.   One could expand this compound component by adding bill-of-materials generation, adding features to support material-resource planning (MRP), and adding support for complex work-breakdown structures (WBSs).

2.3.1 Production Request

Guided tour. The production-request component is shown in Figure 2-36. The production-request component has one pink moment-interval, production request.

Production request. A pink production request links to a yellow manufacturing-process manager. It might be a grouping of some number of other production requests. It also links to pink production-request detail(s).

Production-request detail. A pink production-request detail specifies the quantity that is needed and when it is needed. It links to a blue material-resource production description, indicating what needs to be produced.

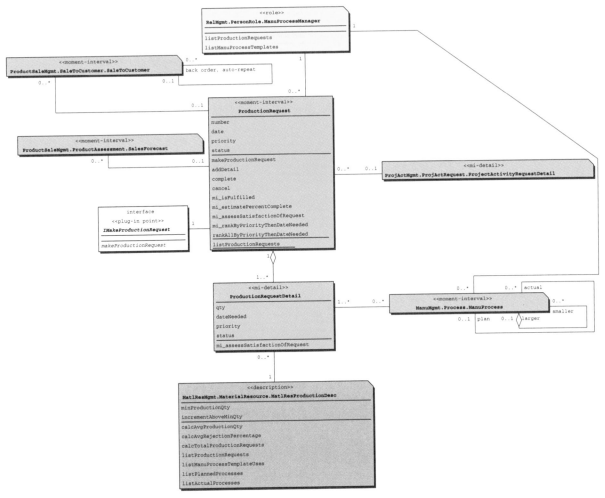

FIGURE 2-36. ▲ Production-request component.

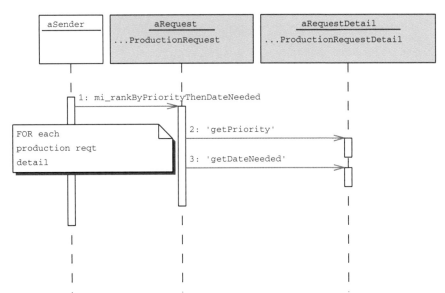

FIGURE 2-37. ▲ Rank by priority then by date needed.

Before and after. For production request, the preceding pink moment-intervals are sale to customer, sales forecast, and project-activity request detail. For production-request detail, the subsequent pink moment-interval is a manufacturing process, more specifically a manufacturing-process plan (one with actual dates and times).

Methods. Key methods include: make production request, rank requests by priority and then by date needed, generate planned process starting at, and assess satisfaction of a request.

Interactions. The "rank by priority then by date needed" sequence is shown in Figure 2-37. A sender asks a pink production request to rank its details by priority, then by date. A production request asks each of its pink details for its priority and date needed, so it can sort the result and return it to the sender. (Note the class method with a similar name, "rank all by priority then date needed.")

2.3.2 Manufacturing-Process Template

Guided tour. The manufacturing-process-template component is shown in Figure 2-38. The process-template component has one central blue description, manufacturing-process template.
    A template uses relative times; a plan uses actual dates and times.

Manufacturing-process template. A blue manufacturing-process template may consist of a number of smaller templates, steps for getting a job accomplished. In fact, a manufacturing-process template might be part of some number of larger templates, making that smaller template a step in some larger processes. So a template could be for an overall

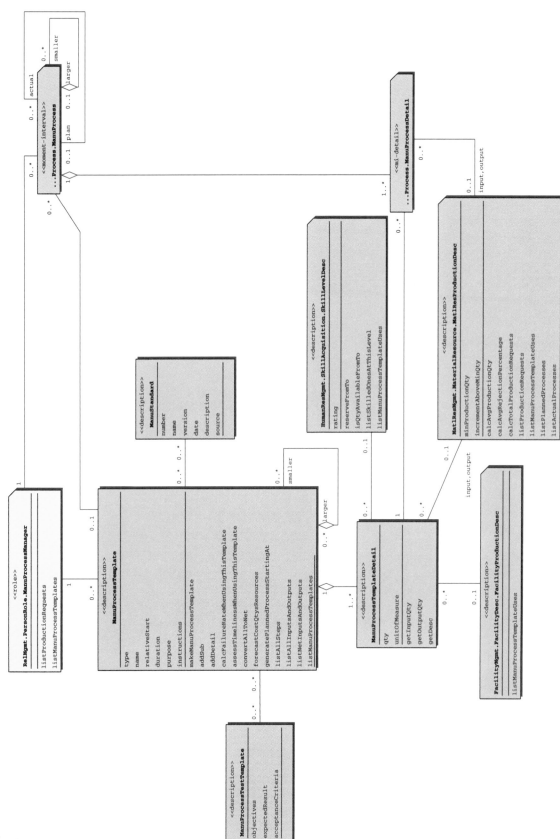

FIGURE 2-38. ▲ Manufacturing-process-template component.

process, a step within another process, or both (in different contexts). (This is the reason why we did not model both "manufacturing-process template" and "manufacturing-process template step," preferring instead to model just the former, using an aggregation link to, in effect, model the latter.)

Tip. Series of aggregation links? Try modeling the upper-level classes in the series as a single class, with an aggregation link connecting one object to others in the same class. Use a sequence diagram to show how it works. This approach often simplifies a model without any loss of expressiveness.

In this case, here's how it works (Figure 2-39): A template asks its smaller templates to list all of its steps, each smaller template asks each of its even smaller templates to list all of its steps, and so on.

Back to the guided tour! A blue manufacturing-process template links to a yellow manufacturing-process manager. It also links to a blue manufacturing standard and blue test template(s).

Manufacturing-process detail. A blue manufacturing-process detail specifies the quantity and units of measure of something needed in a manufacturing process, big or small. It links to a number of blue descriptions, indicating a material resource, facility, or human resource (skill level) required.

Before and after. For manufacturing-process template, the subsequent pink moment-interval is manufacturing process.

Methods. Key methods include: make manufacturing-process template, generate planned process starting at, list net inputs and outputs, assess timeliness when using this template, and calculate failure rate using this template.

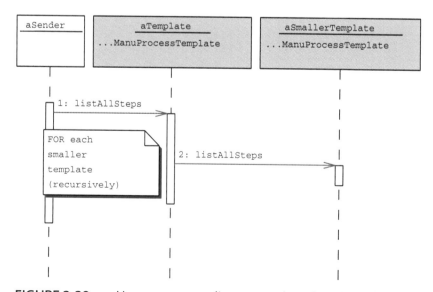

FIGURE 2-39. ▲ Use a sequence diagram to show how it works.

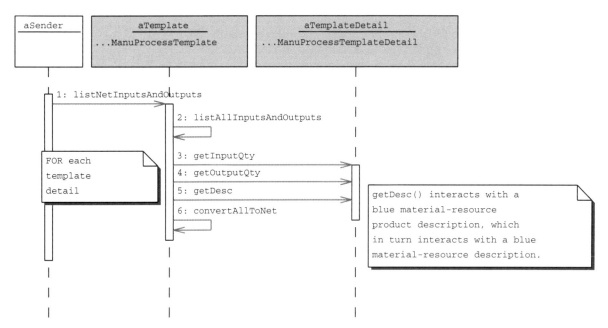

FIGURE 2-40. ▲ List net inputs and outputs.

Interactions. The "list net inputs and outputs" sequence is shown in Figure 2-40. (Net inputs and outputs are the overall inputs and outputs, not including the output-to-input flows occurring within its sub-templates.) A sender asks a blue template to list its net inputs and outputs. To begin with, the template invokes its "list *all* inputs and outputs" method. That method iterates through the template and its sub-templates, getting input and output quantities and descriptions. Then the "convert *all* to net" method balances inputs and outputs, coming up with a list of net inputs and outputs. The template returns the result to the sender.

2.3.3 Manufacturing Process

Guided tour. The manufacturing-process component is shown in Figure 2-41. The manufacturing-process component has one pink moment-interval, manufacturing process.

Manufacturing process. A pink manufacturing process links to a yellow manufacturing-process manager, a manufacturing-process execution manager, and a process inspector. It links to some yellow facility-in-use roles, each of which links to a green facility (within the facility component). It also links to pink manufacturing-process detail(s).

A pink manufacturing process links to other manufacturing-process objects. It links to larger and smaller processes (using aggregation).

Also, a pink manufacturing process links from a planned process to some number of actual executions of that process.

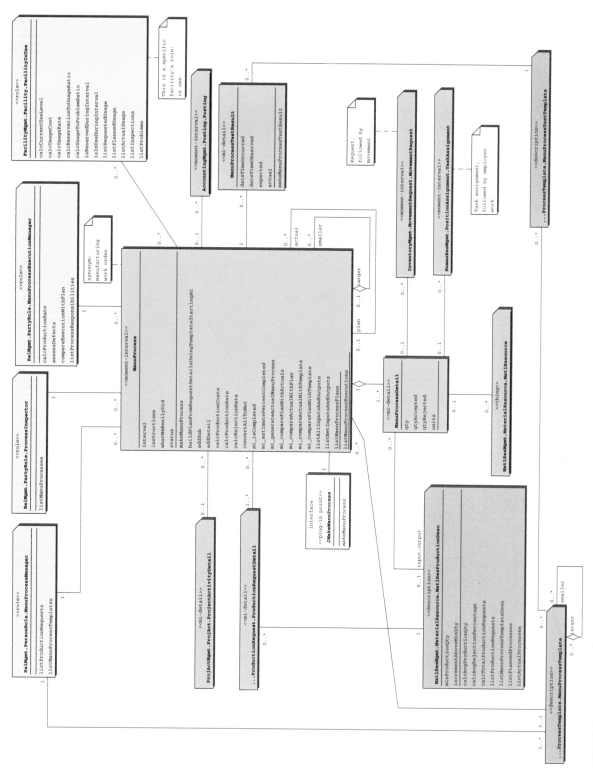

FIGURE 2-41. ▲ Manufacturing-process component.

▲ 77

Tip. Template, plan, then actual? Model with one template class and one plan/actual class. Link a template to plans, then each plan to actual(s). Label the link ends "plan 0..1" and "actual 0..*."

Manufacturing-process detail. A pink manufacturing-process detail specifies a quantity of something within this manufacturing process. It links to a movement request (to move material resources; movement follows request, within the movement component). Or it links to a task assignment (to assign human resources; employee work follows assignment, within the employee-assignment component).

Look at the link between manufacturing process and manufacturing-process test result. A pink manufacturing process might have some number of pink manufacturing-process test results.

Manufacturing-process test result. A pink manufacturing-process test result captures the various test results during a manufacturing process. It links to a manufacturing-process test template.

Before and after. For manufacturing process, the preceding pink moment-intervals are some number of production-request details. For example, you might group a production-request detail for 1,000 chocolate bars (in one set of requests) with a production-request detail for 5,000 chocolate bars (in another set of requests).

For manufacturing process, the subsequent pink moment-interval is accounting posting. For manufacturing-process detail, the subsequent moment-intervals are movement request and task assignment.

Methods. Key methods include: make manufacturing process, build plan from request details using template starting at, calculate quantities produced, compare plan with actual (to see how good the plan is), compare actual with plan (to see how closely the actual follows the plan), compare actual with template, and compare plan with template.

Tip. Compare two objects with each other? Better: let one of the two compare itself to the other. This keeps related things together and makes reuse much more likely.

Interactions. The "build plan from request details using template starting at" sequence is shown in Figure 2-42. A sender asks a pink plan process to fill in itself using given request details, a template, and a start time. The process asks the template for the values it needs; the process sets its own values accordingly. Then the process asks a template for a smaller template; the process gets the values it needs; and the process adds a smaller process to itself. (Each process builds its own details too; we did not show those interactions in the diagram.) At the end, the pink process returns the plan to the sender.

2.3.4 Supervisory Control and Data Acquisition (SCADA)

Guided tour. The SCADA component is shown in Figure 2-43. Now we look at Supervisory Control and Data Acquisition (SCADA, as it's known

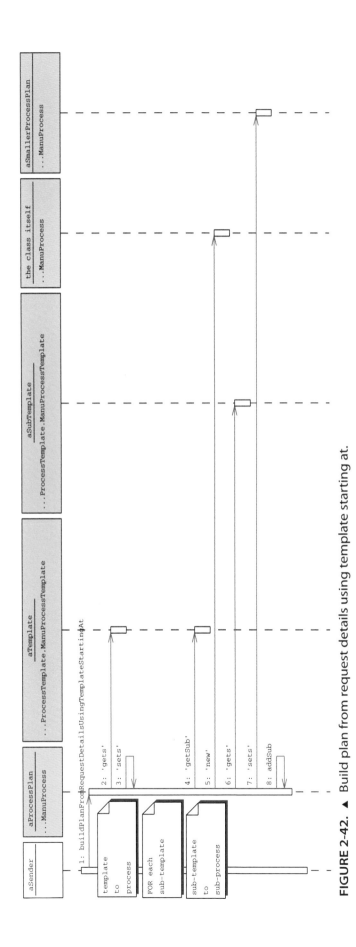

FIGURE 2-42. ▲ Build plan from request details using template starting at.

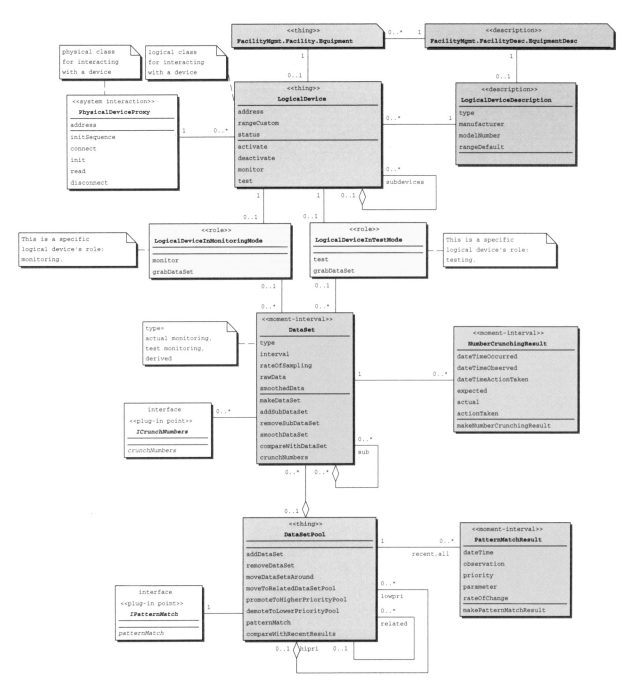

FIGURE 2-43. ▲ SCADA component.

in manufacturing circles). The SCADA component has four key classes: logical device, physical-device proxy (a system-interaction class), data set, and data-set pool.

A *logical device* encapsulates the logical layer for interacting with a physical-device proxy.

A *physical-device proxy* encapsulates the physical layer for interacting with the physical device.

Tip. Interacting with another system or a device? Model a logical class (a problem-domain boundary for your system) and a physical proxy class (a system-interaction class).

Logical device. A green logical device links to logical sub-devices, providing behavior across the collection of logical sub-devices. It links to a corresponding blue logical-device description. It links to its yellow roles, "logical device in monitoring mode" and "logical device in test mode."

When a green logical device messages one of its roles, it sends itself along as an argument. Then the yellow role asks the logical device for its physical-device proxy and then interacts with it directly.

Data set. A pink data set provides number-crunching behavior for that data set. It links to sub-data sets, providing behavior across the collection of sub-data sets. It links to a yellow "logical device in monitoring mode" or to a "logical device in test mode." A data set links to pink number-crunching result(s), a history of results derived from a data set. A pink data set also links to a green data-set pool.

Data-set pool. A green data-set pool provides number-crunching behavior for a collection of data sets. It links to higher priority data sets, lower priority data sets, and to related data sets. It also links to pink pattern-match result(s), a history of its pattern-match observations.

Methods. Key methods include: activate/monitor/test/deactivate a logical device, crunch numbers, pattern match, and promote/demote/move a data set to another data-set pool.

Interactions. The "activate logical device" sequence is shown in Figure 2-44. A sender asks a green logical device to activate itself. The logical device invokes its "set status" method, setting the status to "monitor." A separate thread within the logical device object recognizes the operational state change (to "monitor"). It asks its yellow monitoring role to begin monitoring, passing along its corresponding physical-device proxy object. The role asks the physical-device proxy to connect and initialize. The physical-device proxy interacts with the physical device. Then the role asks the proxy to read a data set; the role asks the pink data set class to create a new object in that class, and the role asks that object to establish itself as a data set, given the arguments the role passes along to it. The role continues busily working away, until a sender asks the logical device to do something other than monitor (which in turn notifies the role).

Note that the yellow role is responsible for its own on-going behavior. It acts, rather than waits to be polled. Now the physical-device proxy, interacting with a relatively dumb physical device, might need to continually poll. And that is fine. Within your model, letting objects act on their own behalf tends to keep attributes and methods that work on them closer together—a good thing.

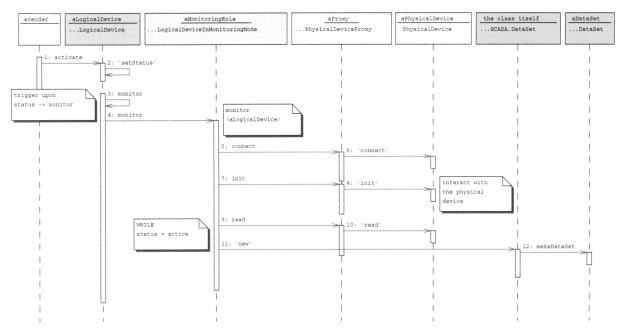

FIGURE 2-44. ▲ Activate a logical device and begin monitoring.

Tip. Polling within your model? No. Let your objects do their own things, reporting only as needed. (A physical-device proxy polls a physical device if it needs to.)

Interactions. The "pattern match" sequence is shown in Figure 2-45. A sender asks a green data-set pool to do some number crunching. So a data-set pool invokes its plug-in algorithm, passing itself as an argument. The number-crunching algorithm coordinates the work to be done. For example, it might get a pink data set, send it to another data set and ask it to compare itself with the other. It might also compare what it finds with its list of recent pink pattern-match results; it could record its own pattern-match results. It might do more, like connect data sets, merge data sets, combine data sets into a new overall data set with the original data sets as sub-data-sets, and so on. At the end, the data-set pool returns control to the sender.

2.4 INVENTORY MANAGEMENT

What. Inventory management is moving and storing inventory into, out of, and between storage units.

Scope. Inventory management begins with defining the storage units and ends in inventory movements.

Steps. First, define storage units. Second, accept movement requests. Third, combine those requests into planned movements (also known as pick lists). Fourth, move inventory.

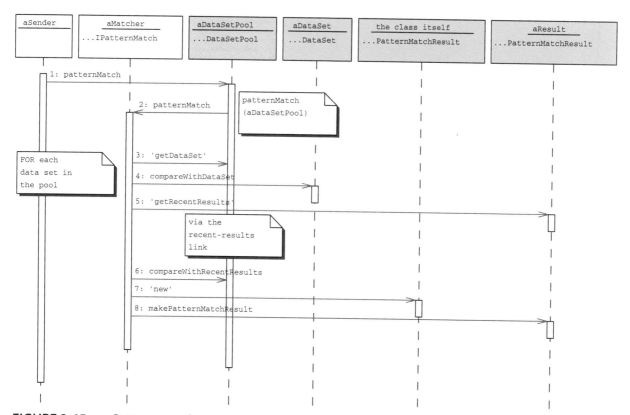

FIGURE 2-45. ▲ Pattern match.

Links. Track the material resources in storage units (materials-resource management). Track the products in storage units (product-sale management).

Mirror images. Here, we move things into the business. In product-sales management, we move things out of the business.

Components. The components within inventory management are (Figure 2-46):

- Storage unit
- Movement request
- Movement

Moment-intervals. The main moment-intervals for inventory management are (Figure 2-47):

- Quantity on hold
- Movement request
- Movement

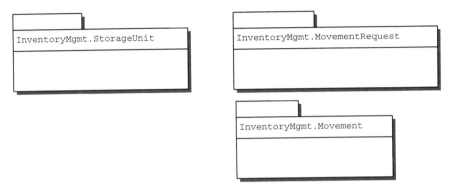

FIGURE 2-46. ▲ Inventory-management components.

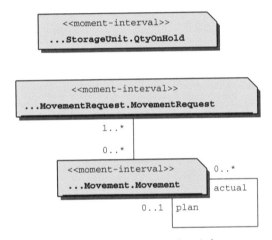

FIGURE 2-47. ▲ Summary in pink.

Interactions. The components work together to get things done. An example of intercomponent interaction, "compare request with actual movements," is shown in Figure 2-48. A sender asks a pink movement request to compare itself with subsequent actual movements. A request asks each of its request details. Each request detail asks its corresponding planned movement detail for its actual movement detail. Finally, the request detail interacts with the actual movement detail, comparing requested vs. actual movement. At the end, a movement request returns the assessment to the sender.

Expansion. One could expand this compound component planning vehicle movement, automating inventory movement, tracking and billing when goods on consignment at a customer site are consumed by a customer, and adding more complex inventory valuation calculations.

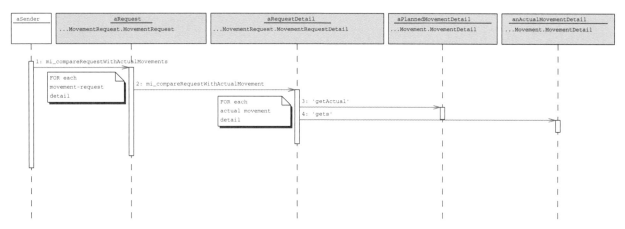

FIGURE 2-48. ▲ Compare request with actual movements.

2.4.1 Storage Unit

Guided tour. The storage-unit component is shown in Figure 2-49. The storage-unit component has one pink moment-interval, quantity on hold. Yet the real focus of this component is the green storage unit. A storage unit represents a place where things are stored. Examples of a storage unit are bin, shelf, aisle, section, loading dock, warehouse, a collection of warehouses, or a work position in an assembly line.

Storage unit. A green storage unit links to a yellow stock manager and a storage-unit owner (we include the latter for tracking inventory stored at a supplier site or a customer site). It also links to a blue storage-unit description, for its standard storage-unit description (for example, the standard dimensions for a certain kind of bin). A storage unit links to larger and smaller storage units. And storage unit links to its green storage-unit detail(s).

Storage-unit detail. A green storage-unit detail tracks the quantity of some kind of content in that storage unit. It links to a blue material-resource quantity description. It links to some number of green material resources. It also links to some number of pink quantity-on-hold objects.

Quantity on hold. A pink quantity-on-hold object knows how much is on hold and until when. It links to a movement requester, the one who requested the hold. It links to a blue material-resource quantity description, for putting a quantity on hold, no matter what storage unit it is in. Or it links to green storage-unit detail(s), indicating that the quantity on hold is reserved from those storage units in particular (for example, from a specific warehouse).

Methods. Key methods include: add quantity of content, remove quantity of content honoring holds (both storage content holds and storage-unit-specific holds), and move quantity of content honoring holds (meaning, storage-unit-specific holds).

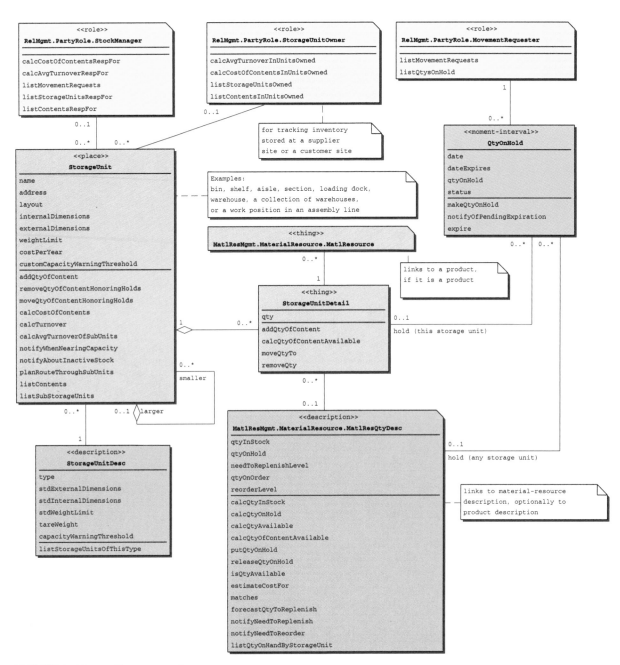

FIGURE 2-49. ▲ Storage-unit component.

Interactions. The "remove a quantity of content from a storage unit, honoring holds" sequence is shown in Figure 2-50. A sender asks a green storage unit to remove a quantity of content, honoring holds. A storage unit asks its green storage-unit details to calculate the quantity of content available. The storage-unit detail asks its blue material-resource quantity

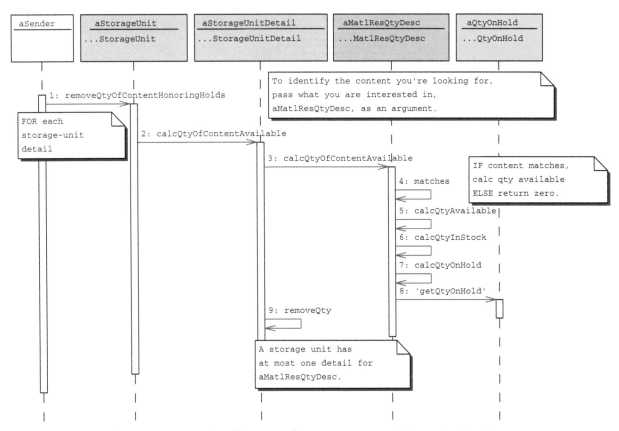

FIGURE 2-50. ▲ Remove a quantity of content from a storage unit, honoring holds.

description to calculate the quantity available. A material-resource quantity description checks to see if the content is a match. If so, it calculates the quantity available (quantity in stock minus quantity on hold) and returns the result; otherwise, it simply returns zero. A storage-unit detail removes what it can and then returns the amount removed to the storage unit. At the end, the green storage unit returns the quantity removed to the sender.

2.4.2 Movement Request

Guided tour. The movement-request component is shown in Figure 2-51. The movement-request component has one pink moment-interval, movement request.

Movement request. A pink movement request links to a yellow movement requester and a stock manager. It also links to pink movement-request detail(s).

Movement-request detail. A pink movement-request detail specifies the quantity to be moved and its priority. It also links to a green storage-unit detail.

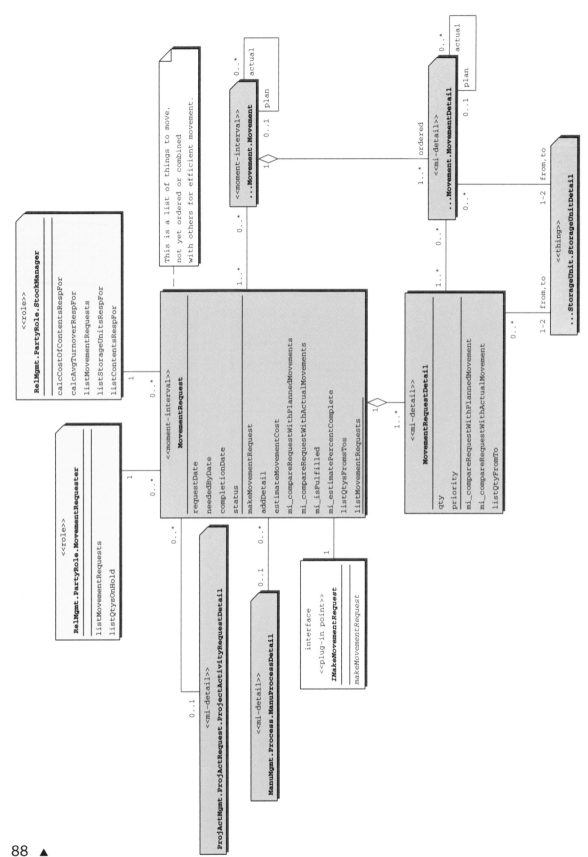

FIGURE 2-51. ▲ Movement-request component.

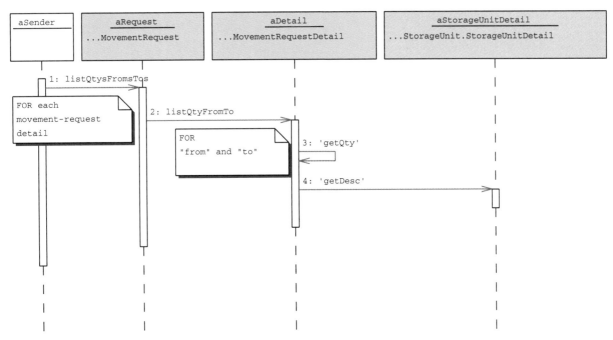

FIGURE 2-52. ▲ List quantities from to.

Before and after.   For movement request, the preceding pink moment-intervals are project-activity request detail and manufacturing-process detail. The subsequent pink moment-interval is movement.

Methods.   Key methods include: make movement request, list quantities from to, and compare request with actual movements.

Interactions.   The "list quantities from to" sequence is shown in Figure 2-52. A sender asks a pink movement request to list its from's and to's. The movement request asks its pink movement-request detail(s) to list its quantity, "from" description, and "to" description. A detail asks its storage-unit detail for its description. At the end, the movement request returns the result to the sender.

2.4.3 Movement

Guided tour.   The movement component is shown in Figure 2-53. The movement component has one pink moment-interval, movement.

Movement.   A pink movement links to a yellow picker. It links from a planned movement to an actual movement(s). A planned movement links to actual movement(s).

Movement detail.   A pink movement detail specifies the quantity moved. A movement detail links to a green storage-unit detail.

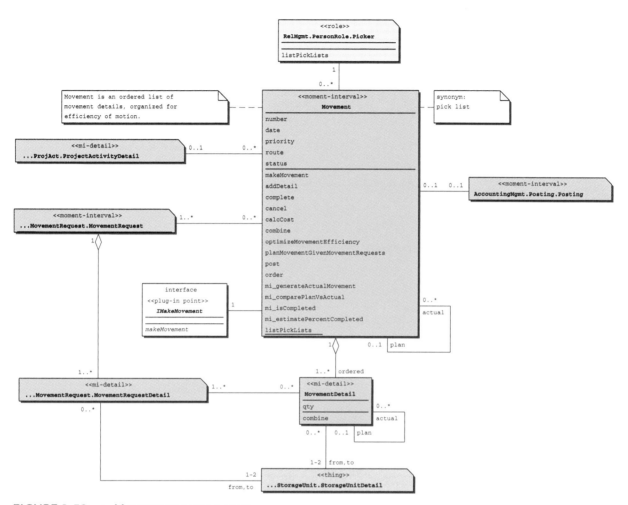

FIGURE 2-53. ▲ Movement component.

Before and after. For movement, the preceding pink moment-intervals are movement request and project-activity detail (in project-activity management). The subsequent pink moment-interval is accounting posting.

Methods. Key methods include: make movement, plan movement given movement request(s), and optimize movement efficiency.

Interactions. The "plan movement given movement requests" sequence is shown in Figure 2-54. A sender asks a pink movement to build a plan, given some number of movement requests. The movement asks for a pink movement-request's details and translates them into movement details. Then the movement iterates across its pink movement details, maximizing efficiency of motion (by combining movements and ordering them). At the end, the movement returns control to the sender.

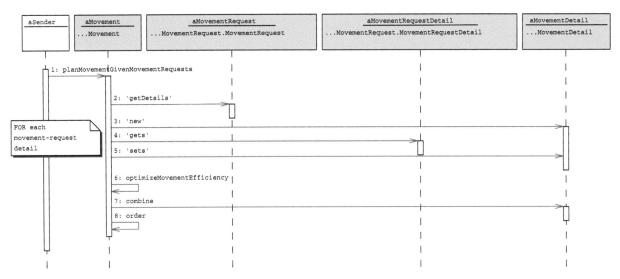

FIGURE 2-54. ▲ Plan movement given movement requests.

3 Sell

This chapter presents three compound components:

1. Product-sale management, for businesses that collect payments by issuing invoices to customers and (eventually) getting paid
2. Cash-sale management, for businesses that collect payment at the time of a sale
3. Customer-account management

3.1 PRODUCT-SALE MANAGEMENT

What. For flexibility, we treat a product as a material resource with some added responsibilities. In this way, we can take any material resource and turn it into a product (this happens in some industries).

A product can be a product in the traditional sense, a service, or a combination of both.

Product-sale management supports the selling of products (goods, services, or combination of both)—on an invoicing basis, rather than on a "cash and carry" basis (as in cash-sales management).

Scope. Product-sale management starts with sales and ends with invoicing.

Steps. First, define product types and products. Second, make a sale to a customer. Third, ship products. Fourth, invoice the customer. Fifth, record the delivery of products; track and resolve delivery-problem reports. Sixth, make agreements and assessments.

Links.   Deduct quantity from inventory (link with material-resource management; it interacts with inventory management). Post invoice totals (accounting management).

Mirror images.   In product-sales management, we move things out of the business on an invoicing basis (from us to a customer). In material-resource management, we move things into the business on an invoicing basis (from a supplier to us).

Components.   The components within product-sale management are (Figure 3-1):

- Product
- Sale to customer
- Shipment to customer
- Delivery to customer
- Invoice to customer
- Product agreement
- Product assessment

Moment-intervals.   The main moment-intervals for product-sale management are (Figure 3-2):

- Product price
- Sale to customer
- Shipment to customer
- Delivery to customer
- Delivery-problem report
- Invoice to customer
- Discount agreement

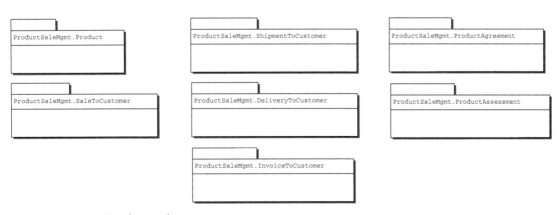

FIGURE 3-1. ▲ Product-sale management components.

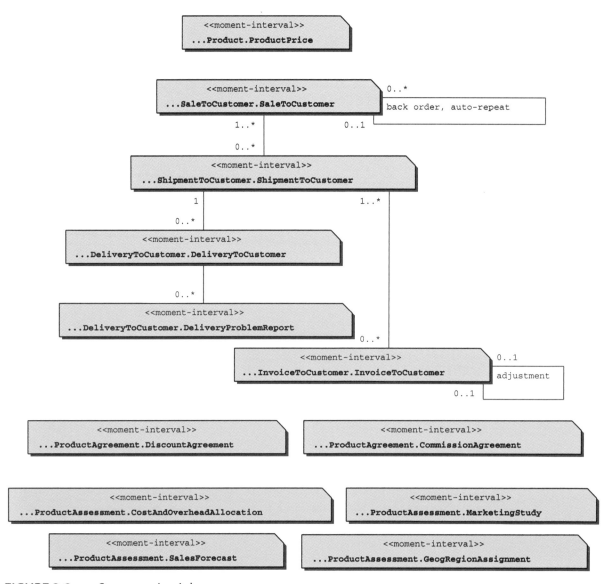

FIGURE 3-2. ▲ Summary in pink.

- Commission agreement
- Cost and overhead allocation
- Marketing study
- Sales forecast
- Geographic-region assignment

Interactions. The components work together to get things done. An example of inter-component interaction, "calculate direct commissions for a sales rep," is shown in Figure 3-3. A sender asks yellow sales rep to

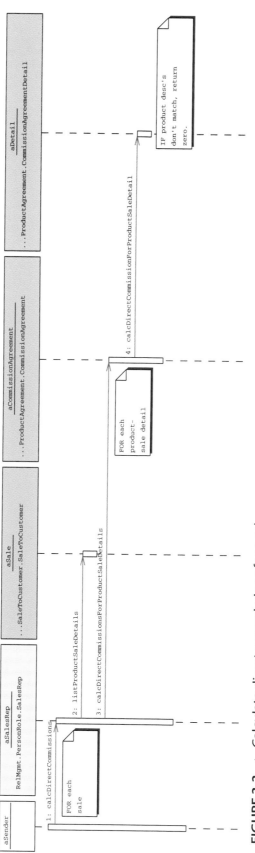

FIGURE 3-3. ▲ Calculate direct commissions for a sales rep.

calculate its commissions, the ones coming from its own sales (called "direct" commissions). A sales-rep object asks each of its pink sales to build a list of product-sale details. Next, a sales-rep object asks each of its pink commission objects to calculate direct commissions. A commission object then matches its product descriptions and quantities with the sales details, looking for a valid match, then computes the commission for the sales of that product. Some commission objects might not be linked to a product description, in which case that commission applies across all of the product-sale details. At the end, the sales rep returns its results to the sender.

Expansion. One could expand this compound component by adding components to support pre-sales activities, including customer and prospect rankings, test marketing activities and results, and feature tracking for future products. One could also expand it with post-sale activities including service.

3.1.1 Product

Guided tour. The product component is shown in Figure 3-4. The product component has two central classes: a green product and a blue product description.

Product. A green product is something that a business sells, is individually identifiable (it has a serial number), and is something that must be individually tracked. If a product were not individually identifiable, you would not need a green thing; instead, you could use a quantity of a blue catalog-entry-like description. Even if something were individually identifiable, if all you needed to track were quantities rather than each numbered unit itself, then again a quantity of a blue catalog-entry-like description would be sufficient. If you need to track more than just quantity, e.g., specific serialized items, then you need to manage a collection of these items. The green product could have a collection of serial numbers, or a blue catalog-entry-like description could have a collection of green serialized products.

A green product has required links to a green material resource and a blue product description. A blue product description has a required link to a blue material-resource description.

For example, consider a specific Ford F-100 truck, identifiable by its serial number, called a vehicle identification number. A green product linked to a green material-resource represents it.

Now consider a standard catalog-entry that applies to any Ford F-100 on a dealer's lot: the manufacturer is Ford, the model name is F-100, the vehicle type is truck, and so on. A blue product linked to a blue product description represents it.

A green product links to some yellow product-being-sold roles.

Product description. This is a catalog-entry-like description of a kind of material resource. A blue material-resource description is the main description; it links to a number of other supporting blue context-specific

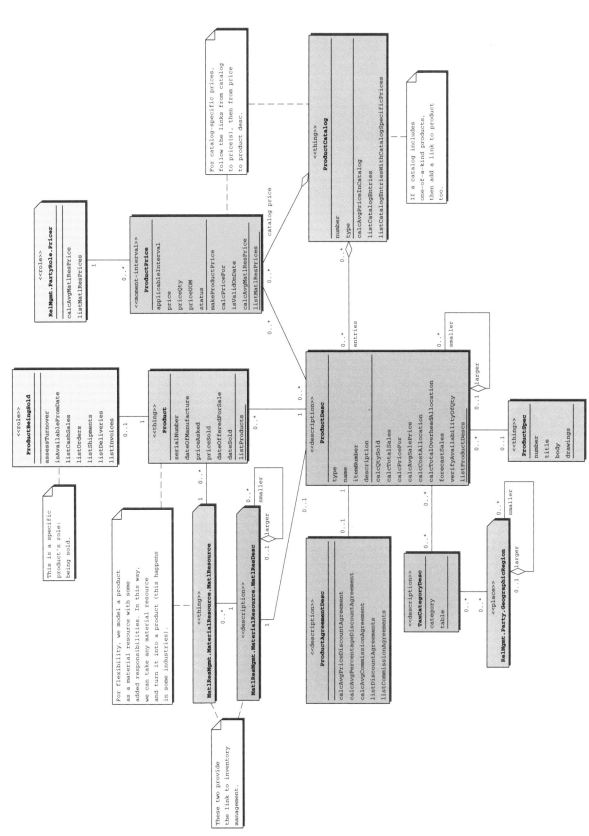

FIGURE 3-4. ▲ Product component.

supplemental descriptions that one can add as needed. Notice that the blue tax category links to its applicable green geographic regions.

Other components use certain quantities of a product description. For example, if someone requests 20 Ford F-100 trucks, then a component might include a request detail with a quantity of 20, linked to a blue product description that applies to each Ford F-100.

Product price.   A pink product price sets a price for a quantity and price unit of measure, applicable for an interval of time. It links to blue product description(s) or to green products. It also links to the yellow pricer responsible for setting that price.

You have some modeling choices when it comes to price. You can model it as an attribute in the green product (for example, the price for that red Ferrari, that one right there!) or a blue description (for example, the price of a Snickers bar of a particular size). However, if you want to track that price in the past (for trend analysis), in the present (to make sales), and in the future (planning for forthcoming price changes), then yes, you need a pink moment-interval for product price.

Tip.   An attribute? Or something more? If you need an attribute value, use an attribute. If you need to track the change in that value over time (past, present, future), use a pink moment-interval. If you need to set that value once and then apply it to other objects as a standard, use a blue description.

Product catalog.   A green catalog is a collection of blue product descriptions. If the catalog were a catalog of one-of-a-kind collectibles, it would link to green product(s) too. In addition, if a catalog were to have catalog-specific prices, then a catalog would link to its pink prices, with those prices linking to its product descriptions.

Tip.   Track values for each link? Add a pink moment-interval. Just need to categorize links? Use this simpler approach: label the endpoint of the link with the categories.

Methods.   Key methods include: calculate price for a detail object (with quantity and unit of measure), list catalog entries with catalog-specific prices, and verify availability of a quantity.

Interactions.   The "calculate price for a detail object (with quantity and unit of measure)" sequence is shown in Figure 3-5. A sender asks a blue product description to calculate its price, given a detail object, one with values for both quantity and unit of measure. The product description asks each of its pink product price(s) to calculate its price for a detail— and goes with whatever is the best price. (In a retail system, the "best price" might be the lowest price. In an insurance system, it might be the highest price. Insurance-application developers know what we mean! A business always looks different when standing on the other side of the counter.) A product price checks that it's valid for the date, gets the price, gets the quantity, gets the price unit of measure, asks the detail object for its price, asks the detail object for its unit of measure, does the math, and

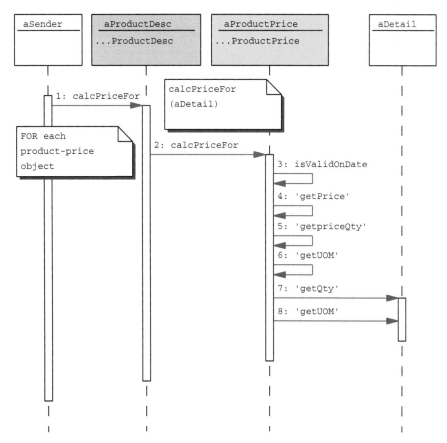

FIGURE 3-5. ▲ Calculate price for a detail object (with its quantity and unit of measure).

returns its result. At the end, the product description returns the price to the sender.

Another interesting interaction sequence is "list catalog entries with catalog-specific prices," shown in Figure 3-6. A sender asks a green product catalog to list its catalog entries with catalog-specific prices. The product catalog asks each of its pink product prices for its corresponding blue product descriptions. Then it interacts with both the product price and the product descriptions, adding to its list of catalog entries with prices. At the end, the product catalog returns the list to the sender.

3.1.2 Sale to Customer

Guided tour. The sale-to-customer component is shown in Figure 3-7. The sale-to-customer component has one pink moment-interval, sale to customer.

Sale to customer. A pink sale-to-customer links to two yellow roles: sales rep and customer. It links to a green (ship-to) address and a green terms-and-conditions object. It also links to pink sale-to-customer detail(s).

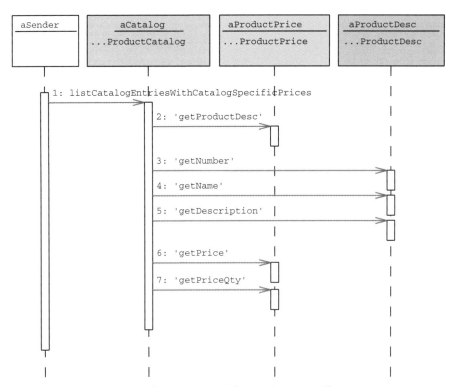

FIGURE 3-6. ▲ List catalog entries with catalog-specific prices.

Sale-to-customer detail. A pink sale-to-customer detail specifies quantity, negotiated price, and status. It links to a blue product description. Or it might link to yellow product-being-sold roles, which in turn link to green products (in the product component). It might link to a green (ship-to) address.

Before and after. For sale to customer, the subsequent pink moment-interval is shipment to customer.

Methods. Key methods include: make sale to customer, calculate the total of a sale, calculate quantity of a product description sold over an interval, and compare sale with deliveries.

Interactions. The "calculate quantity sold" sequence is shown in Figure 3-8. A sender asks a blue product description to calculate the quantity sold, passing along an applicable interval as an argument. The product description asks each of its pink sale details for its quantity within that interval. Each sale detail then asks its pink sale for its date, checks to make sure it's within the interval, then returns its amount (if within the interval) or zero (otherwise) to the product description. Ultimately, the product description returns its result to the sender.

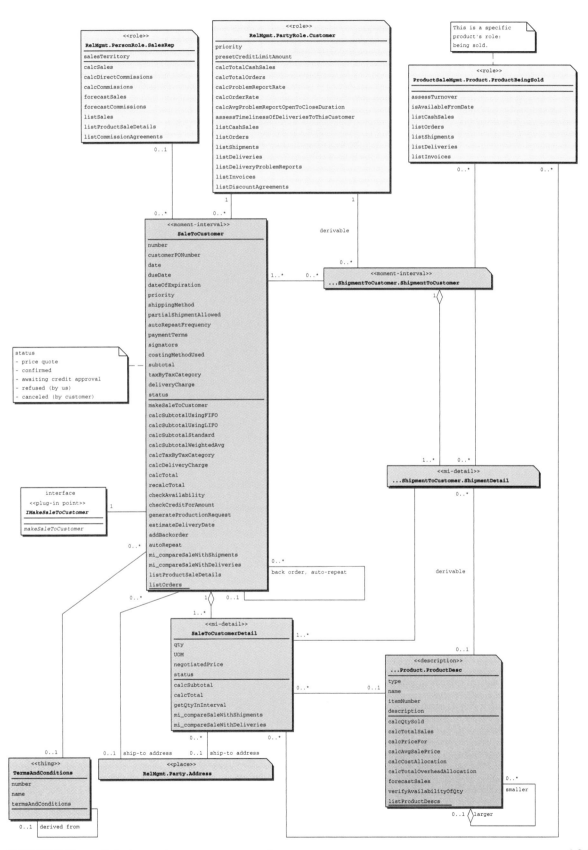

FIGURE 3-7. ▲ Sale-to-customer component.

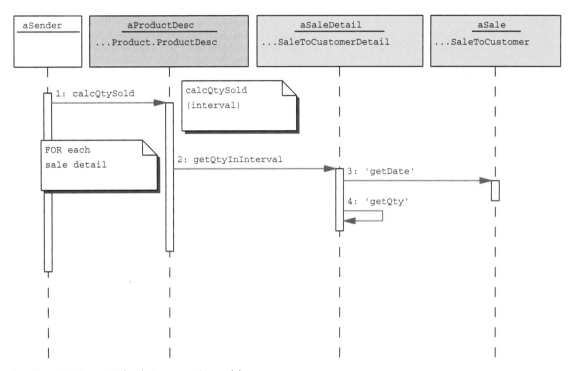

FIGURE 3-8. ▲ Calculate quantity sold.

3.1.3 Shipment to Customer

Guided tour. The shipment-to-customer component is shown in Figure 3-9. The shipment-to-customer component has one pink moment-interval, shipment to customer.

Shipment to customer. A pink shipment to customer links to a yellow customer (a derivable link, via sale); it links to a yellow shipper too. It also links to pink shipment detail(s).

Shipment detail. A pink shipment detail specifies a quantity shipped. A shipment detail links to a blue product description (derivable, by traversing links back to sale detail); or it might link to some number of yellow product-being-sold roles, each of which links to a green product (in the product component).

Before and after. For shipment to customer, the preceding pink moment-interval is sale to customer. The subsequent pink moment-interval is delivery to customer.

Methods. Key methods include: make shipment to customer, verify if credit is still acceptable, calculate shipment weight, assess deviation from sales, and compare shipment with deliveries.

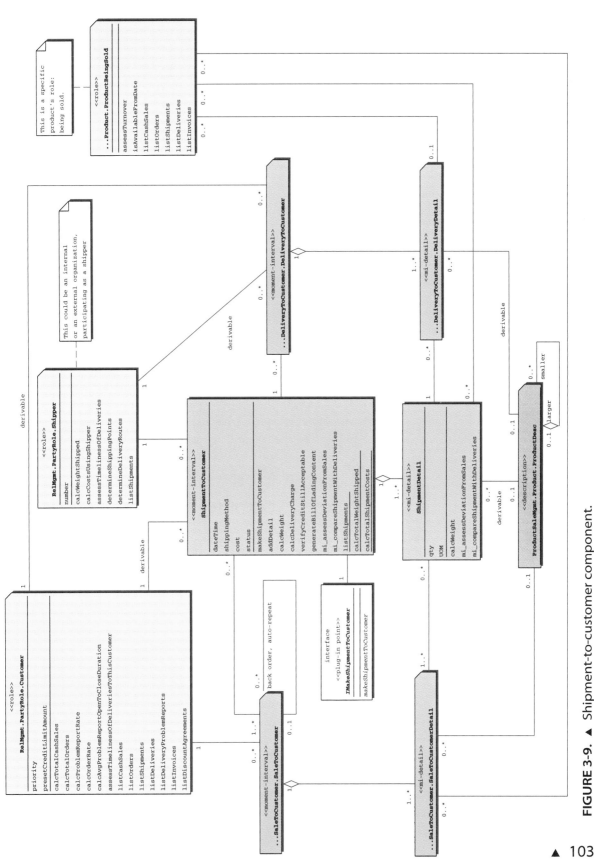

FIGURE 3-9. ▲ Shipment-to-customer component.

▲ 103

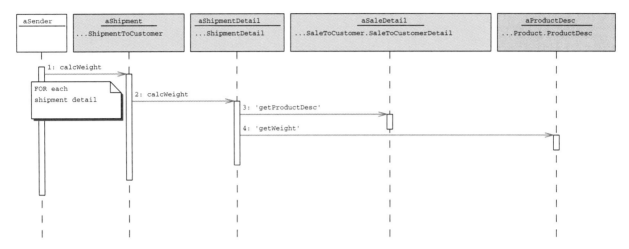

FIGURE 3-10. ▲ Calculate shipment weight.

Interactions.   The "calculate shipment weight" sequence is shown in Figure 3-10. A sender asks a pink shipment to calculate its weight. A shipment then asks each pink shipment detail to calculate its weight. Each shipment detail asks its corresponding pink sale detail for its connecting blue product-description. Finally, it asks the product description for its weight, multiplies weight by the shipment-detail quantity, and returns the total weight for the shipment detail. Shipment adds up the results and returns the total to the sender.

3.1.4 Delivery to Customer

Guided tour.   The delivery-to-customer component is shown in Figure 3-11. The delivery-to-customer component has two pink moment-intervals, linked together: delivery to customer and delivery problem report.

Delivery to customer.   A pink delivery-to-customer links to a yellow customer (a derivable link, via shipment and sale). It links to some yellow product-being-sold roles, each of which links to a green product (in the product component). It also links to pink delivery detail(s).

Delivery detail.   A pink delivery detail specifies quantities received and quantity returned. A delivery detail links to a blue product description (derivable, by traversing links back to sale detail); or it might link to some number of yellow product-being-sold roles, each of which links to a green product (in the product component).

Delivery problem-report.   A delivery may result in some number of pink problem-reports. Each problem-report tracks when it's opened and closed, along with other relevant information.

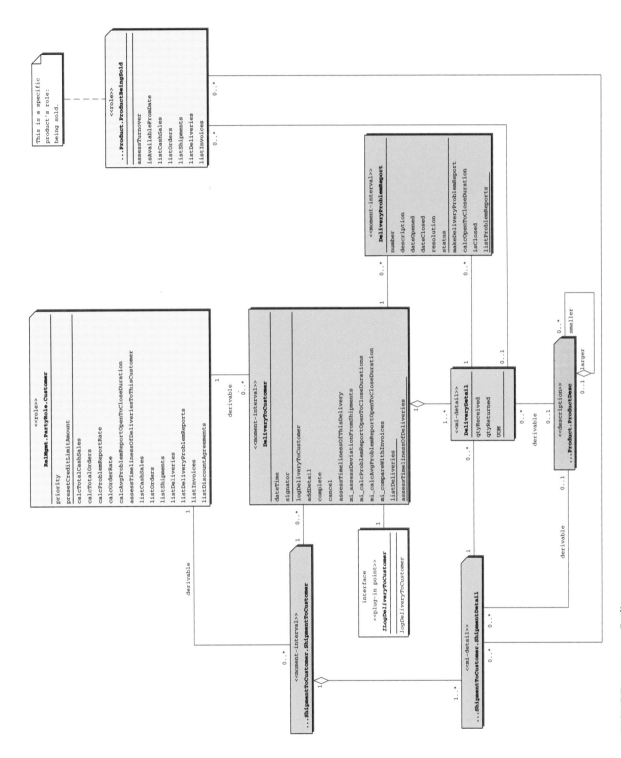

FIGURE 3-11. ▲ Delivery-to-customer component.

▲ 105

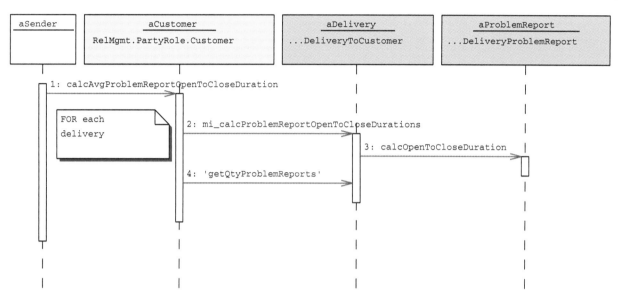

FIGURE 3-12. ▲ Calculate average open-to-close problem-report duration.

Before and after. For delivery-to-customer, the preceding pink moment-interval is shipment-to-customer.

Methods. Key methods include: log delivery to customer, assess timeliness of this delivery, and calculate the average problem report open-to-close duration for a customer.

Interactions. The "calculate average open-to-close problem-report duration" sequence is shown in Figure 3-12. A sender asks a yellow customer to calculate its open-to-close problem-report duration. It asks each of its pink delivery(ies) to calculate its own problem-report open-to-close duration. Each delivery asks each of its pink delivery-problem reports to calculate its own open-to-close duration. A customer totals the duration, asks each delivery for its quantity of problem reports, performs the math, and returns the result to the sender.

3.1.5 Invoice to Customer

Guided tour. The invoice-to-customer component is shown in Figure 3-13. The invoice-to-customer component has one pink moment-interval, invoice to customer.

Invoice to customer. A pink invoice to customer links to a yellow customer. It also links to pink invoice detail(s).

Invoice detail. A pink invoice detail tracks the quantity, price, and unit of measure. An invoice detail links to a blue product description (derivable,

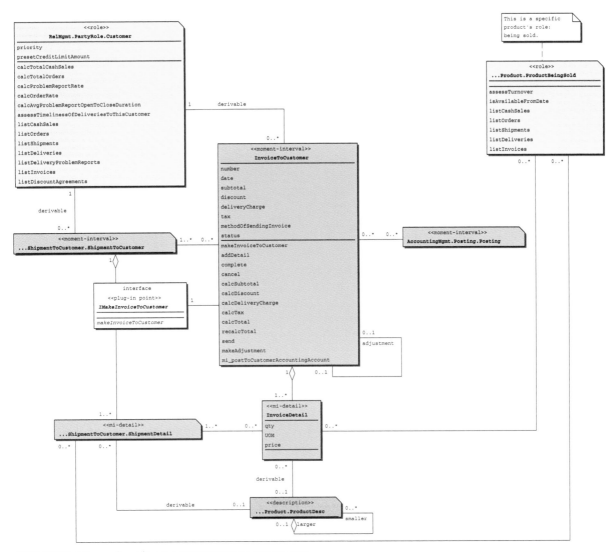

FIGURE 3-13. ▲ Invoice-to-customer component.

by traversing links back to sale detail); or it might link to some number of yellow product-being-sold roles, each of which links to a green product (in the product component).

Before and after. For invoice to customer, the preceding pink moment-interval is shipment. The subsequent pink moment-interval is accounting posting.

Methods. Key methods include: make invoice to customer, calculate the total of an invoice, and make an adjustment invoice.

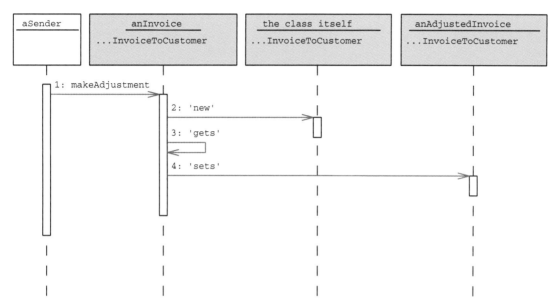

FIGURE 3-14. ▲ Make an adjustment invoice.

Interactions. The "make an adjustment invoice" sequence is shown in Figure 3-14. A sender asks a pink invoice to make an adjustment invoice. The pink invoice does so in two steps: First, it asks the invoice class for a new invoice object. Then it gets its own values and sets the new invoice object accordingly.

Tip. Track different versions? Make a copy, copy its parts, and link the original to the copy. After that, use a "diff" (difference) method to identify what has changed. Alternative: keep the original and track each change (sometimes simpler).

3.1.6 Product Agreement

Guided tour. The product-agreement component is shown in Figure 3-15. The product-agreement component has two pink moment-intervals: discount agreement and commission agreement.

Discount agreement. A pink discount agreement links to a yellow customer. It also links to pink discount-agreement detail(s).

Discount-agreement detail. A pink discount-agreement detail specifies a discount, applicable to sales of products described by certain blue product-agreement descriptions (if linked) or to sales of any products (otherwise).

Commission agreement. A pink commission agreement links to a yellow sales rep. It links to a green "node linked within a commission agreement." It also links to pink commission detail(s).

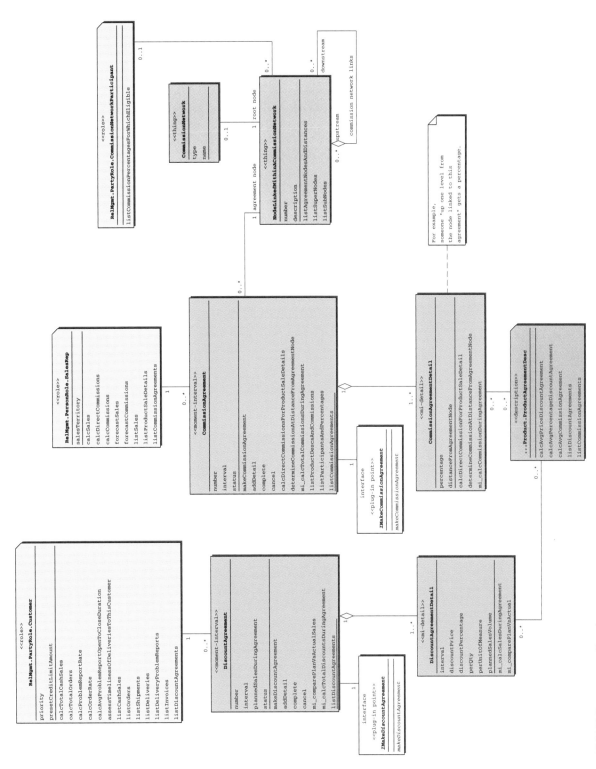

FIGURE 3-15. ▲ Product-agreement component.

Commission-agreement detail.　A pink commission-agreement detail specifies a commission, applicable to sales of products described by certain blue product-agreement descriptions (if linked) or to sales of any products (otherwise).

Commission network.　Commission agreements define who gets a commission from a sale. When a sales rep makes a sale, he earns a commission. Others in a commission network, for example, the sales rep's managers, rippling upwards several levels, each enjoy commission from that sale. A green commission network links to the root node for a given network. A green "node linked within a commission network" might link to a commission agreement, making it a so-called "agreement node," the node from which indirect commission will be calculated. A green "node linked within a commission network" might also link to a yellow commission-network participant, indicating the assignment of a party to a particular node within a commission network (note that this assignment could change, without affecting the shape of the commission network).

Methods.　Key methods include: make discount agreement, make commission agreement, and list commission percentages for which eligible.

Interactions.　The "calculate direct commissions" sequence is shown in FIgure 3-16. A sender asks a yellow sales-rep object to calculate its direct commissions. For each of its sales, the sales-rep object asks for a list of pink product-sale details. Then it sends the product-sale details to its pink commission agreement(s). Each commission agreement sends each product-sale detail to its pink commission-agreement details, which in turn calculate whatever commission is due (for the product description or product being sold role) linked to that sale detail. Eventually, the sales-rep object tallies up the commissions and returns the result to the sender.

3.1.7 Product Assessment

Guided tour.　The product-assessment component is shown in Figure 3-17. The product-assessment component has four pink moment-intervals: cost-and-overhead allocation, marketing study, sales forecast, and geographic-region assignment.

Cost-and-overhead allocation.　A pink cost-and-overhead allocation links to a yellow accountant. It also links to blue product description(s).

Marketing study.　A pink marketing study links to a yellow marketer. It also links to pink marketing-study detail(s), tracking specifics within a study. A pink marketing-study detail tracks part of a marketing study, optionally linked to blue product description(s).

Sales forecast.　A pink sales forecast links to a yellow marketer. It might link to some number of green geographic regions. It also links to pink sales-forecast detail(s), tracking specifics within a forecast. A pink

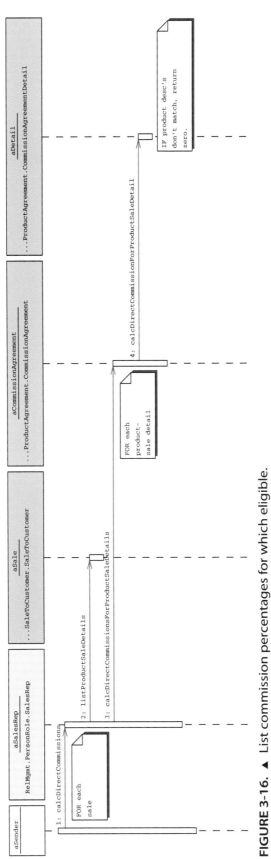

FIGURE 3-16. ▲ List commission percentages for which eligible.

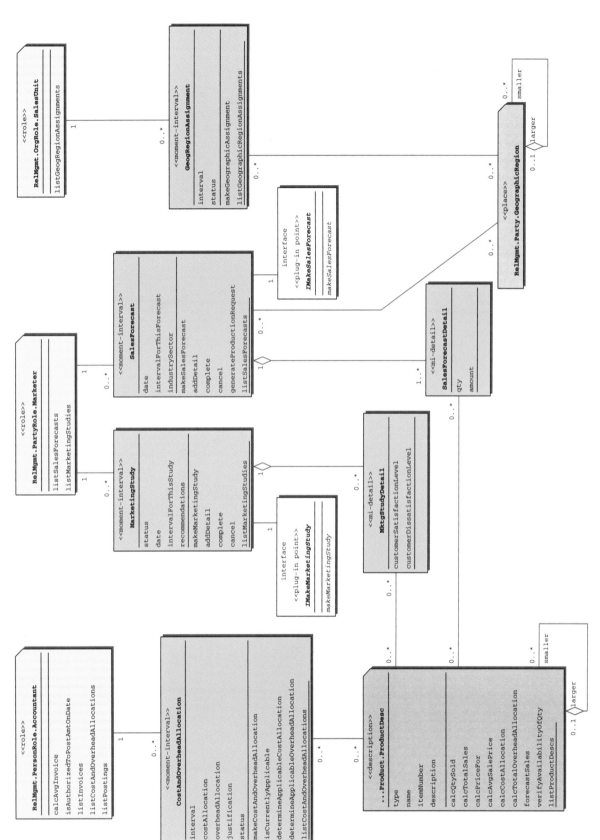

FIGURE 3-17. ▲ Product-assessment component.

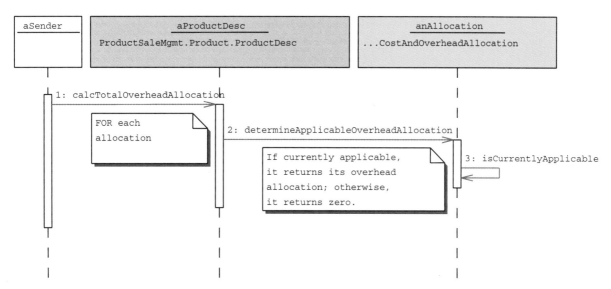

FIGURE 3-18. ▲ Calculate total overhead allocation.

sales-forecast detail tracks part of a sales forecast, optionally linked to blue product description(s).

Geographic-region assignment.   A pink geographic-region assignment links to a yellow sales unit, which in turn links to a green organizational unit (in the party component). It might link to some number of geographic regions.

Methods.   Key methods include: make cost and overhead allocation, make a marketing study, make a sales forecast, and make a geographic-region assignment, and calculate total overhead allocations.

Interactions.   The "calculate total overhead allocation" sequence is shown in Figure 3-18. A sender asks a blue product description to calculate its total overhead allocation. It asks each of its pink cost-and-overhead allocations to determine its applicable overhead allocation. If it is currently applicable, an allocation returns its overhead number; otherwise, it simply returns zero. The product description adds up the results and returns the total to the sender.

3.2 CASH-SALE MANAGEMENT

What.   Cash-sale management supports the selling of products (goods, services, or combination of both) on a "cash and carry" basis, rather than on an invoicing basis (as in product-sales management). Retail businesses often run on a "cash and carry" basis; that's whom this component is for.

Scope. Cash-sale management begins with a cash-drawer assignment and ends with cash sales (includes sale items, return items, or both).

Steps. First, establish cash-drawer assignments. Second, start a cash-sale session, a working session. Third, make cash sales.

Links. Track the products sold (product-sale management, which in turn interacts with material-resource management and finally inventory management). Post sales and payments (accounting management).

Mirror images. Here, payment is immediate. In product-sales management, payments come in over time.

Components. The components within cash-sale management are (Figure 3-19):

- Cash-sale session
- Cash sale

Moment-intervals. The main moment-intervals for cash-sale management are (Figure 3-20):

- Cash-drawer assignment
- Cash-sale session
- Cash sale

Interactions. The components work together to get things done. An example of inter-component interaction, "calculate cash-sales rate," is shown in Figure 3-21. A sender asks a yellow cashier object to calculate its cash-sales rate. The cashier object asks each of its pink cash-sale sessions to calculate its cash-sales rate. A session calculates its total by asking each of its pink sales to calculate its total. A session uses the total and its interval to calculate its rate. A cashier object totals the results and returns the rate to the sender.

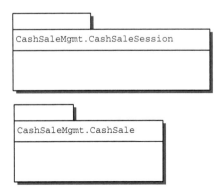

FIGURE 3-19. ▲ Cash-sale management components.

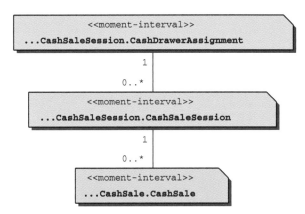

FIGURE 3-20. ▲ Summary in pink.

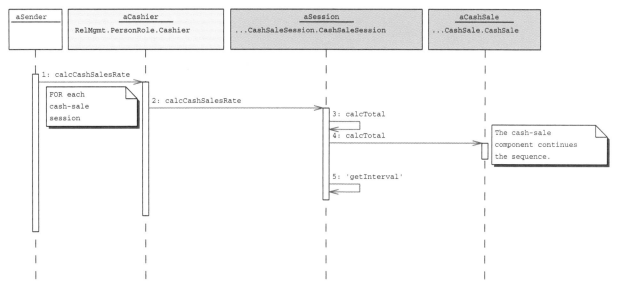

FIGURE 3-21. ▲ Calculate cash-sales rate.

Expansion. One could expand this compound component to accommodate high-volume online cash sales.

3.2.1 Cash-Sale Session

Guided tour. The cash-sale-session component is shown in Figure 3-22. The cash-sale session component has two pink moment-intervals, linked together: cash-drawer assignment and cash-sale session.

Cash-drawer assignment. A pink cash-drawer assignment links to a yellow cashier. It links to a green cash drawer.

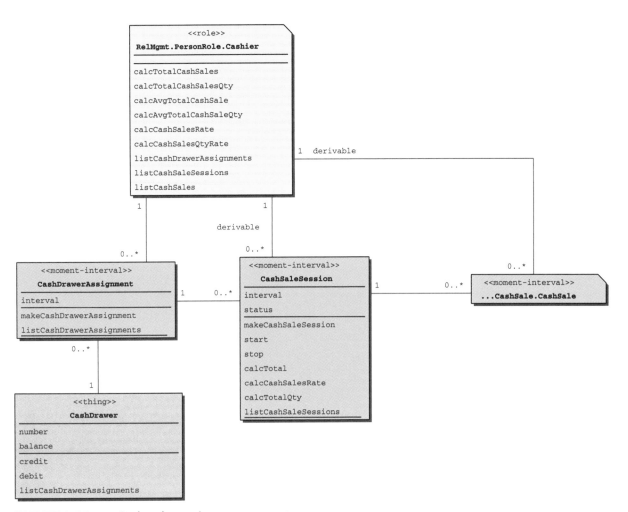

FIGURE 3-22. ▲ Cash-sale-session component.

Cash-sale session.   A pink cash-sale session links to a yellow cashier. Note that this link is derivable, since a cash-sale session *must* link to one cash-drawer assignment *and* each cash-drawer assignment *must* link to one cashier.

A yellow cashier links to some number of cash-drawer assignments. Each cash-drawer assignment links to some number of cash-sale sessions.

The link between cashier and cash-sale session is derivable. The model is fine without it. We occasionally show derived links for increasing modeling understanding. Derived links might or might not be implemented.

Tip.   A link from first to last? If a class links to another, and that one links to another, do you need a link from the first to the last? If the first and the last need to and can associate with each other even without the middle, yes. If not, no (although you could add it and label it "derivable" if it helps in understanding the model).

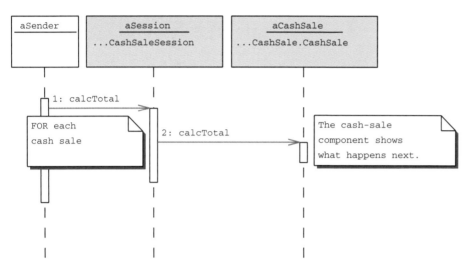

FIGURE 3-23. ▲ Calculate the total of a sale.

Before and after.   For cash-sale session, the subsequent pink moment-interval is cash sale.

Methods.   Key methods include: make cash-sale session, calculate the total cash sales during a session, and calculate a cashier's cash-sales rate.

Interactions.   The "calculate total during a session" sequence is shown in Figure 3-23. A sender asks a pink cash-sale session to calculate its total. The cash-sale session object asks each of its pink cash-sales to calculate its total. (The sequence diagram in the next component shows what happens next.)

3.2.2 Cash Sale

Guided tour.   The cash-sale component is shown in Figure 3-24. The cash-sale component has one pink moment-interval, cash sale.

Cash sale.   A pink cash sale links to two yellow roles: customer and cashier (the cashier link is derivable). It also links to a yellow "facility as business location" (a role played by a green facility, within the facility component). It also links to pink cash-sale detail(s).

Cash-sale detail.   A pink cash-sale detail specifies quantity, unit of measure, and a special price (if one is negotiated) for this line item. A cash-sale detail links to a blue product description. Or it might link to yellow product-being-sold roles, which in turn link to a green product (in the product component).

Before and after.   For cash sale, the preceding pink moment-interval is cash-sale session. The subsequent pink moment-interval is payment.

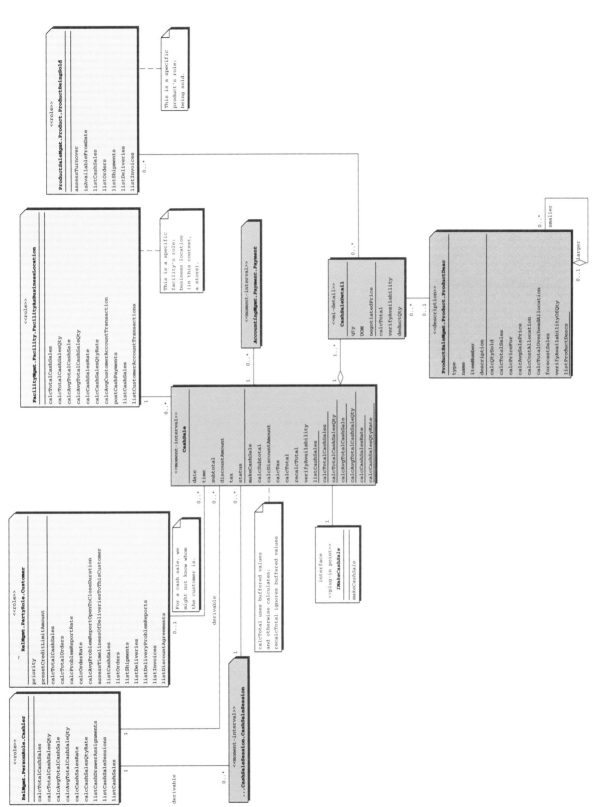

FIGURE 3-24. ▲ Cash-sale component.

Methods.   Key methods include: make cash sale, verify availability, and calculate the total of a sale.

Interactions.   The "calculate the total of a cash sale" sequence is shown in Figure 3-25. A sender asks a pink cash sale to calculate its total. That's a big method; so sale does it by sending a message to each of three steps: calculate subtotal, calculate discount, and calculate tax.

To calculate its subtotal, the cash sale asks each of its pink cash-sale details to calculate its total. A cash-sale detail does this in one of three ways. First, if it has its own value for a negotiated price, it has the total it needs. Second, if it links to a blue product description, it asks it to calculate the price given a quantity and unit of measure. Third, if it links to one or more yellow product-being-sold role objects, it asks each of those objects for a corresponding green product object, and then it asks that object for its price.

The cash sale then calculates the discount, calculates tax, and adds up the total. It returns the result to the sender.

Tip.   Complex method in a sequence-diagram column? Break the method down into smaller steps (using messages that point back to the same object; UML calls them self-delegation messages). Then work out dynamics for each step.

3.3 CUSTOMER-ACCOUNT MANAGEMENT

What.   Many businesses use accounts to track the credits and debits that a customer makes within a given context of dealing with that business. Rental businesses often use accounts to keep track of rentals and returns. Telephone companies use accounts to track credits and debits for telecommunications services. Financial institutions use accounts in perhaps the widest variety of contexts: checking, savings, loans, and various combinations.

Scope.   Customer-account management begins with an application and ends with account transactions.

Steps.   First, accept a customer-account application. Second, evaluate the application. Third, approve or reject it. Fourth, if accepted, generate a new customer account. Fifth, make customer transactions, recording debits, credits, or both.

Links.   Post account transactions (accounting management).

Mirror images.   In customer-account management, we establish and maintain accounts so we can track and present on-going business activity from a customer's perspective. In accounting management, we establish and maintain accounts to track the overall business financially, organized as specified by management, by a regulatory authority (in some countries), or both.

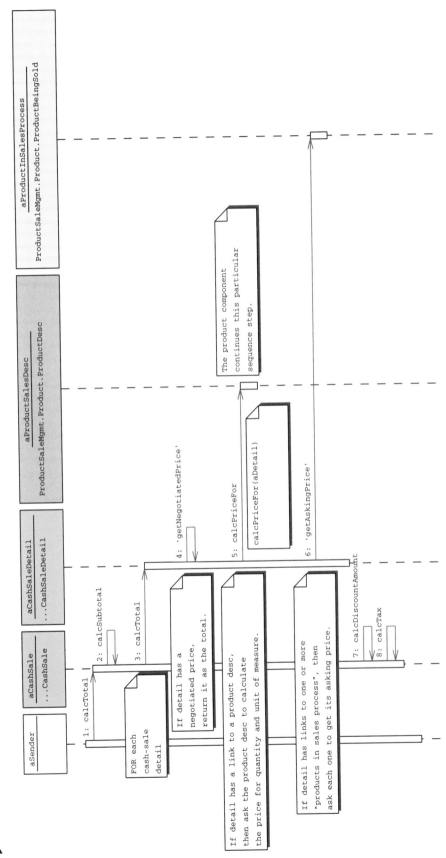

FIGURE 3-25. ▲ Calculate total of a sale.

Components. The components within customer-account management are (Figure 3-26):

- Customer-account application
- Customer account
- Customer-account transaction

Moment-intervals. The main moment-intervals for customer-account management are (Figure 3-27):

- Customer-account application, linked via customer account to
- Customer-account transaction

Interactions. The components work together to get things done. An example of inter-component interaction, "rate an applicant," is shown in Figure 3-28. A sender asks a yellow applicant to rate itself. It gets its credit rating (an attribute value; credit rating could be a pink moment-interval, and credit-rating agency could be a yellow role; yet if all we care about is the current value, then that adds model complexity we don't need).

Also note the attribute in application, credit rating at time of application. Although applicant has its credit rating, that credit rating might change over time. Perhaps we are not interested in how those values change (pink moment-interval) yet we do need to keep the value at the

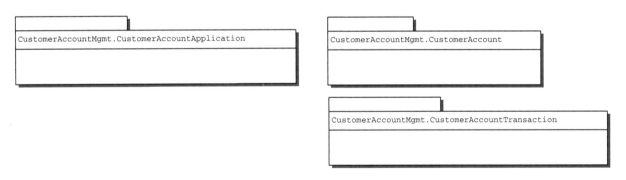

```
CustomerAccountMgmt.CustomerAccountApplication
```

```
CustomerAccountMgmt.CustomerAccount
```

```
CustomerAccountMgmt.CustomerAccountTransaction
```

FIGURE 3-26. ▲ Customer-account management.

```
<<moment-interval>>
...CustomerAccountApplication.CustomerAccountApplication
```

```
<<moment-interval>>
...CustomerAccountTransaction.CustomerAccountTransaction
```

FIGURE 3-27. ▲ Summary in pink.

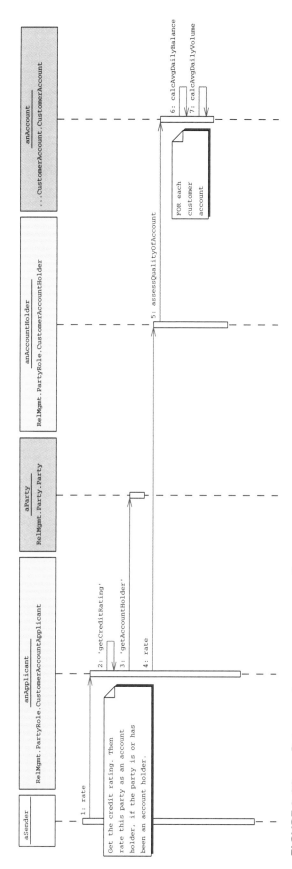

FIGURE 3-28. ▲ Rate a customer-account applicant.

time of the application. That's what the "credit rating at the time of application" attribute is all about.

Tip. Objects linked to a pink moment-interval change over time? If so, add attributes to "snapshot" the objects you need to remember.

The same party participating as an applicant in this context might already be an account holder, a different role. So an applicant asks its green party (in the party component) to get its account holder. As shown in the relationship-management component, a role may be a grouping of other roles. So an applicant role might be a collection of other role-players acting together as an applicant group.

Tip. Send a message from one role to another? Two paths: go through a pink moment-interval. Or if the roles are played by the same person, place, or thing, then go through the common green one instead.

A party returns its yellow account holder (or a null, if no account holder exists).

A yellow applicant asks a yellow account holder to rate itself. The account holder then iterates across its collection of accounts, asking each one to calculate its average daily balance and to calculate its average daily volume (for example, the average daily amount of money flowing in and out of an account).

Expansion. One could expand this compound component by adding methods to scan current account features and suggest additional ones (telephone companies seem very good at this). One could also expand it with financial-service account details (fees, special instructions, discounts, and inter-institution transfers).

3.3.1 Customer-Account Application

Guided tour. The customer-account application component is shown in Figure 3-29. The customer-account application component has one pink moment-interval, customer-account application.

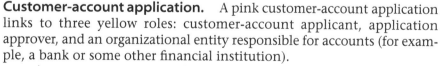

Customer-account application. A pink customer-account application links to three yellow roles: customer-account applicant, application approver, and an organizational entity responsible for accounts (for example, a bank or some other financial institution).

A customer-account application links to a blue customer-account description, indicating the kind of account the application is for. A customer-account application also links to two collections of blue customer-account feature descriptions, selections (of optional features) and additions (of features above and beyond those normally offered for this kind of customer account).

A blue customer-account description links to two collections of customer-account feature descriptions, required features and optional features.

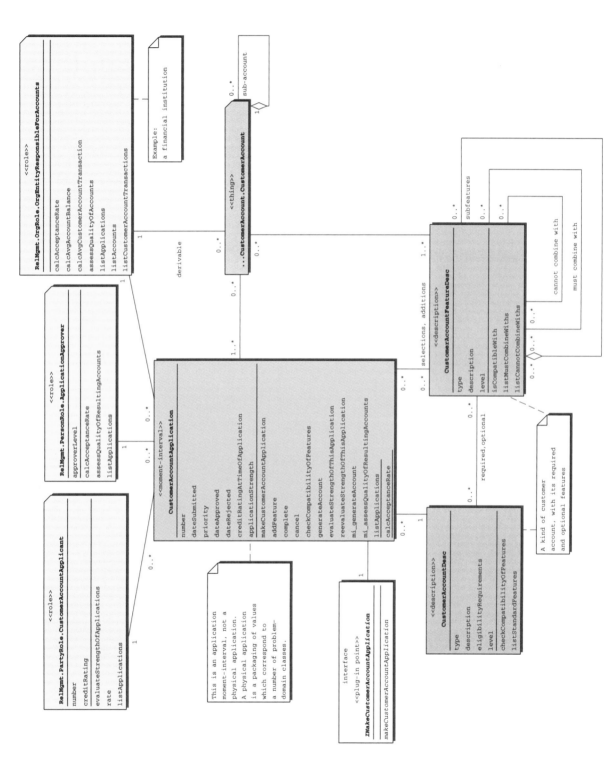

FIGURE 3-29. ▲ Customer-account application component.

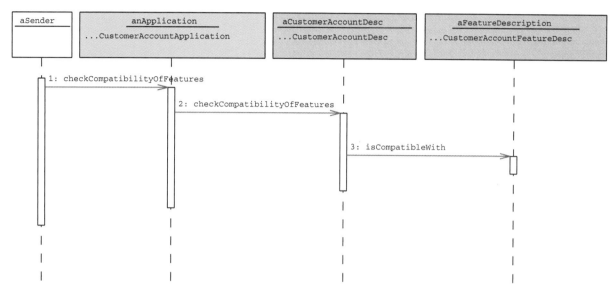

FIGURE 3-30. ▲ Check compatibility of features.

A blue customer-account feature description links to other customer-account feature descriptions, linking to sub-features, "must combine with" features, and "cannot combine with" features.

Before and after. For customer-account application, the subsequent pink moment-interval is customer transaction (via a green customer account).

Methods. Key methods include: make customer-account application, check compatibility of features, generate account, and assess quality of resulting accounts.

Interactions. The "check compatibility of features" sequence is shown in Figure 3-30. (Note: invoke this method after adding or removing a number of features; invoking it with each add or remove results in too many transient errors.) A sender asks a pink customer-account application to check the compatibility of its features. It asks its customer account description, representing the kind of account, to check the compatibility of selected and additional features (passed along as arguments). Finally, a customer-account description interacts with its customer-account feature descriptions, checking for compatibility, including "must combine" and "cannot combine" constraints.

3.3.2 Customer Account

Guided tour. The customer-account component is shown in Figure 3-31. The customer-account component has one green thing, customer account.

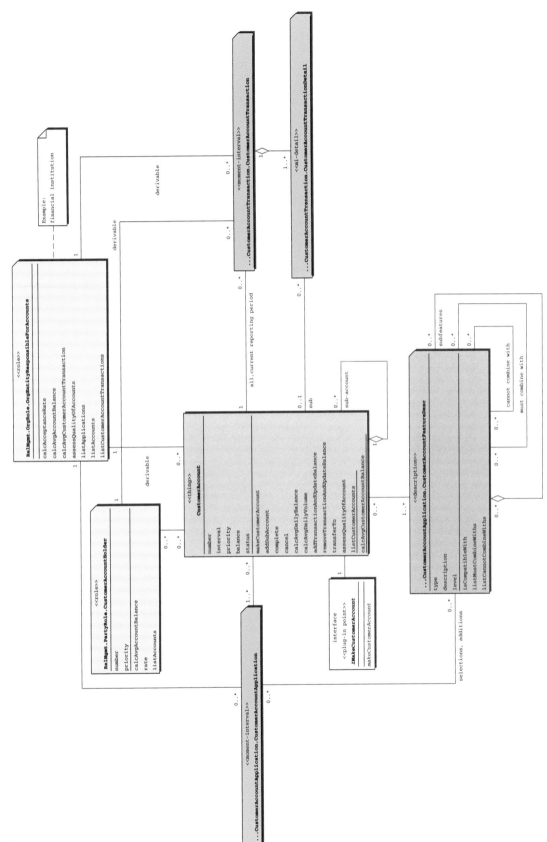

FIGURE 3-31. ▲ Customer-account component.

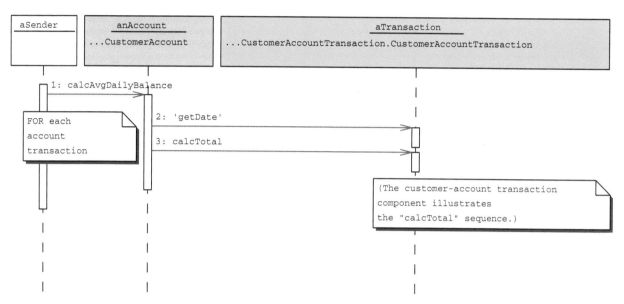

FIGURE 3-32. ▲ Calculate average daily balance.

Customer account.   A green customer account links to two yellow roles, customer-account holder and organizational entity responsible for accounts (derivable via the customer-account application). It also links to one or more blue customer-account feature descriptions.

Before and after.   For customer account, the preceding pink moment-interval is customer-account application. The subsequent pink moment-interval is customer-account transaction (two collections: "all" and "current reporting period").

Methods.   Key methods include: make customer account, calculate average daily balance, and calculate average daily volume (the flow in and out of an account).

Interactions.   The "calculate average daily balance" sequence is shown in Figure 3-32. A sender asks a green account to calculate its average daily balance. It asks each of its "current reporting period" pink transactions for its date and its total, determines the result, and returns it to the sender.

3.3.3 Customer-Account Transaction

Guided tour.   The customer-account transaction component is shown in Figure 3-33. The customer-account transaction component has one pink moment-interval, customer-account transaction.

Customer-account transaction.   A pink customer-account transaction links to three yellow roles: customer-account holder (derivable, via customer account), organizational entity responsible for accounts (derivable,

FIGURE 3-33. ▲ Customer-account-transaction component.

via customer account then customer application), and facility as business location (the location where a given customer-account transaction takes place). It also links to pink customer-account transaction detail(s).

Customer-account transaction detail. A pink customer-account transaction detail specifies a credit (with a positive amount) or a debit (with a negative amount). A customer-account transaction detail links to a green customer account.

Before and after. For customer-account transaction, the preceding pink moment-interval is customer application (via a green account). The subsequent pink moment-interval is an accounting posting of the transaction.

Methods. Key methods include: make customer-account transaction and calculate average customer-account transaction.

Interactions. The "calculate average customer-account transaction" sequence is shown in Figure 3-34. A sender asks a yellow facility as business location to calculate its average customer-account transaction. It asks each of its pink customer-account transactions to calculate its total. A transaction then gets its total and returns it (if a buffered value is present); otherwise it (re)calculates the total by asking each of its pink transaction details for its amount, and then returns the total. Finally, a facility as business location totals it all, gets the number of transactions, calculates the average, and returns the result to the sender.

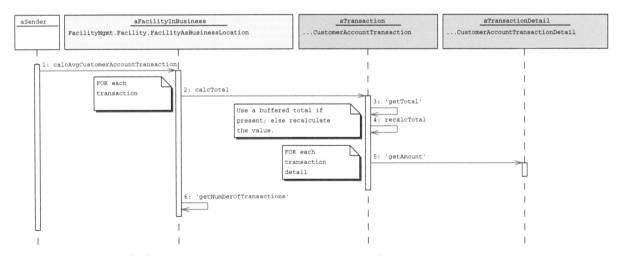

FIGURE 3-34. ▲ Calculate average customer-account transaction.

4 Relate

▶ **Walk this way, talk this way.**

Aerosmith

This chapter presents two compound components:

1. Human-resource management
2. Relationship management

4.1 HUMAN RESOURCE MANAGEMENT

What.   Human resources are the people in the business. Human-resource management is about seeing those people fulfilled in their work assignments and rewarded for the results they produce.

Scope.   Human-resource management begins with a position request and ends with payroll and expense payments.

Steps.   First, make position request. Second, find employees and other candidates. Third, hire new people. Fourth, establish compensation agreements. Fifth, build skills. Sixth, make position assignments. Seventh, make task assignments. Eighth, track employee activity. Ninth, assess performance. Tenth, calculate and pay payroll and expenses.

Links.   Fulfill human resource requests for a project-activity request; complete human resource activities for a project activity (project-activity management). Post payroll and expense payments (accounting management).

Mirror images.   In material-resource management, we move things into the business. In human-resource management, we marshal the people to accomplish results for the business.

Components.   The components within human-resource management are (Figure 4-1):

- Employment
- Position request
- Position assignment
- Work and payment
- Skill acquisition

Moment-intervals.   The main moment-intervals for human-resource management are (Figure 4-2):

- Employment, compensation agreement
- Position request
- Position assignment, task assignment, and performance assessment
- Employee work, payroll payment, and expense payment
- Skill-acquisition program, participation, and skill rating

Interactions.   The components work together to get things done. An example of inter-component interaction, "list qualified candidates for a job," is shown in Figure 4-3. A sender asks a blue job to list qualified candidates. It asks each of its blue skill-level descriptions to find skilled ones at that level. A skill-level description asks its corresponding blue skill description to list skilled ones at a given level. A skill description asks each of its pink skill ratings to list a skilled one at a given level. If the skill level and skill rating values match, then a skill rating object gets the yellow employee-as-resource or applicant and returns it. Ultimately, a job takes the lists it gathers, intersects the lists to come up with a list of qualified candidates, and returns the result to the sender.

Expansion.   One could expand this compound component with added support for employee compensation and benefits.

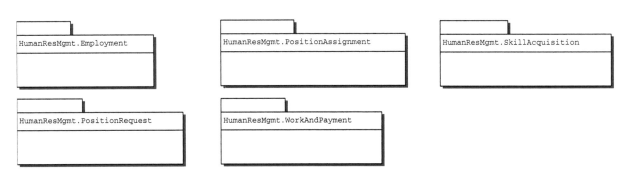

FIGURE 4-1. ▲ Human-resource management components.

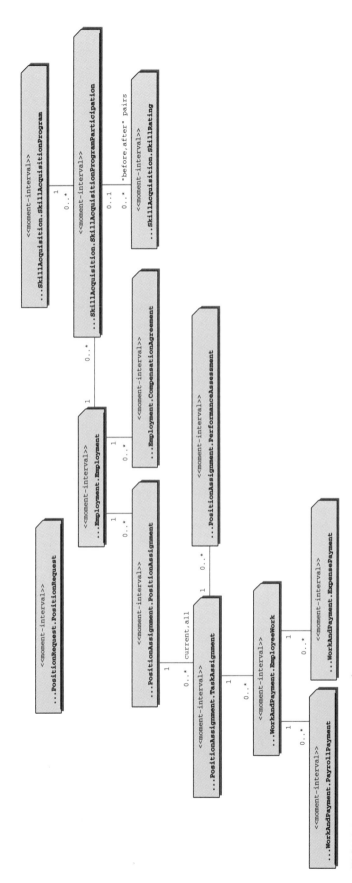

FIGURE 4-2. ▲ Summary in pink.

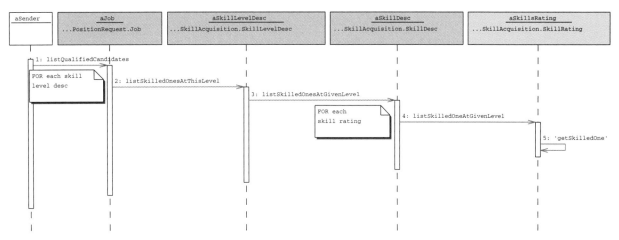

FIGURE 4-3. ▲ List qualified candidates for a job.

4.1.1 Employment

Guided tour. The employment component is shown in Figure 4-4. The employment component has two pink moment-intervals, linked together: employment and compensation agreement.

Employment. A pink employment links to a yellow "employee as compensated one." It also links to a pink compensation agreement.

Compensation agreement. A pink compensation agreement links to three yellow roles: employee as compensated one (derivable), employer as compensation source, and compensation-agreement approver. It also links to pink compensation-agreement detail(s).

Compensation-agreement detail. A pink compensation-agreement detail specifies an amount and its unit of measure. A compensation-agreement detail links to a blue pay-rules description (for example: hourly, no paid overtime). Or it might link to a green benefit account (with a balance), which in turn links to a blue benefit-account description (for example, vacation time).

Before and after. For employment, the subsequent pink moment-intervals are position assignment and skill-acquisition program participation.

Methods. Key methods include: make employment, make compensation agreement, notify when a benefit-account balance reaches its warning-level value, and calculate total compensation.

Interactions. The "calculate compensation defined by a compensation agreement" sequence is shown in Figure 4-5. A sender asks a pink compensation agreement to calculate its compensation (for some interval of

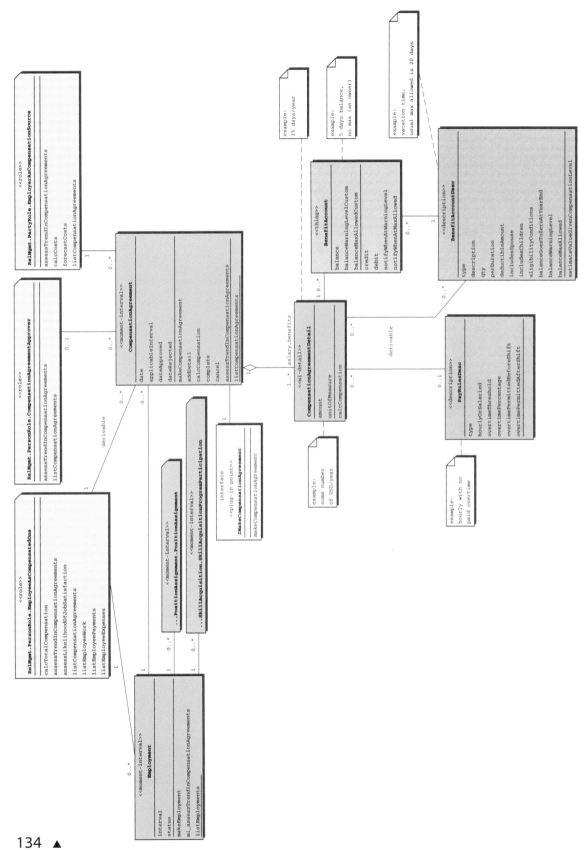

134 ▲

FIGURE 4-4. ▲ Employment component.

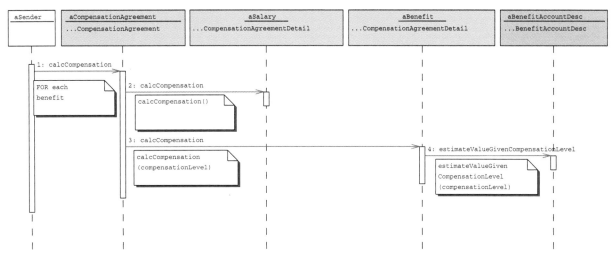

FIGURE 4-5. ▲ Calculate total compensation defined by a compensation agreement.

time). It asks its pink *salary* "compensation agreement details" to calculate its compensation. Then it asks each of its pink *benefit* "compensation agreement details" to calculate the compensation it represents; each benefit asks its corresponding blue benefit-account description to estimate its value given current compensation level. In the end, a compensation agreement object tallies up the numbers and returns its result to the sender.

4.1.2 Position Request

Guided tour.   The position-request component is shown in Figure 4-6. The position-request component has one pink moment-interval, position request.

Position request.   A pink position request links to three yellow roles: position requester, position authorizer, and organization entity with a position to fill. It also links to pink position-request detail(s).

Position-request detail.   A pink position-request detail specifies the quantity and interval (start date-time and end date-time) for one part of an overall request. It links to a blue job. (In effect, a job is what we might otherwise call a "position description.")

Job, skill-level description, and skill description.   A trio of blue descriptions define what skills and skill-levels are required or "nice to have" for a job. Here's an example:

- Job: developer
- Skill level: B (on an ABC scale)
- Skill description: Java programming

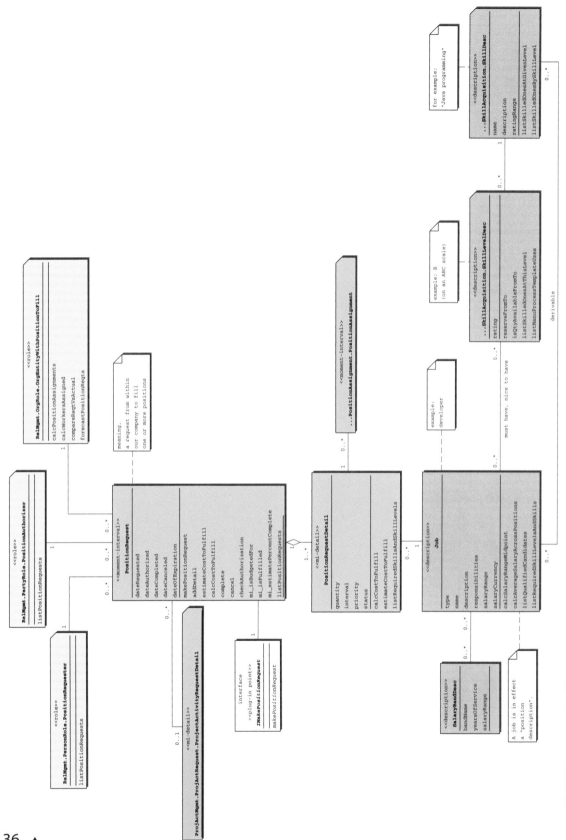

FIGURE 4-6. ▲ Position-request component.

Note that job links to skill level, then skill level links to skill description. This is not a typo! It's the only way to follow the links. Otherwise, if you go from job to skill description, you don't have a way to link to the right skill level for that job.

Tip. Link to a description and an "at this level" description? Link first to the "at this level" description; let the "at this level" description link to the description itself.

To assist model reviewers, we usually add a derivable link, in this case from job to skill description. The other two links are essential, not derivable.

Before and after. For position request, the preceding pink moment-interval is project-activity request detail (in project-activity management). For position-request detail, the subsequent pink moment-interval is position assignment.

Methods. Key methods include: make position request, list required skills and skill levels, and estimate cost to fulfill a position request.

Interactions. The "estimate cost to fulfill a position request" sequence is shown in Figure 4-7. A sender asks a pink position request to estimate the cost to fulfill that request. The request then asks each of its pink request details to estimate its cost. Each pink request detail asks its linking job to calculate its salary-range midpoint, then uses that number plus quantity and interval to calculate a result, and returns it. The request totals the estimate and returns the estimate to the sender.

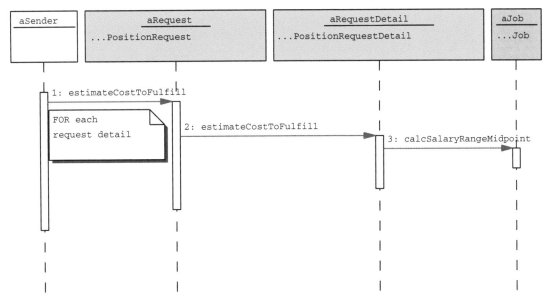

FIGURE 4-7. ▲ Estimate cost to fulfill a position request.

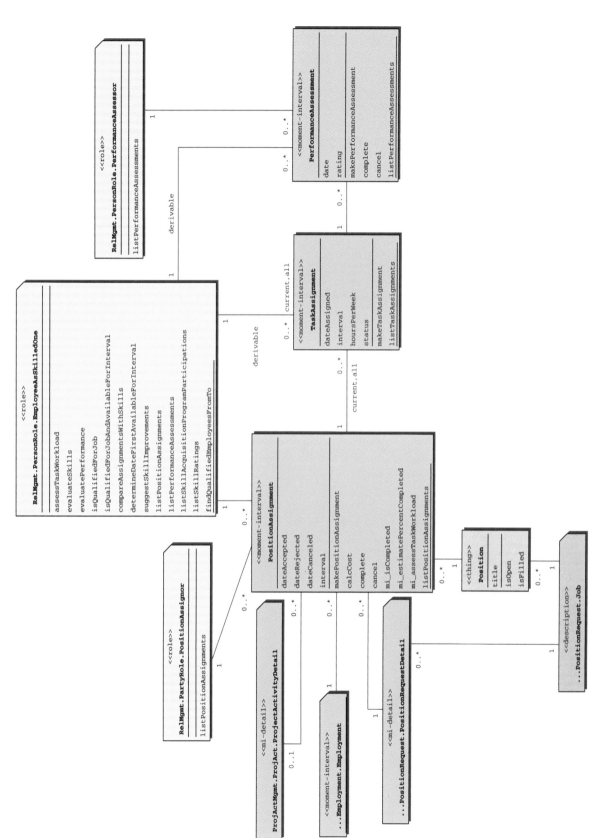

FIGURE 4-8. ▲ Position-assignment component.

4.1.3 Position Assignment

Guided tour. The position-assignment component is shown in Figure 4-8. The position-assignment component has three pink moment-intervals, linked together: position assignment, task assignment, and performance assessment.

Position assignment. A pink position assignment links to two yellow roles: position assignor and employee as skilled one. Position assignment also links to a collection of "all" and "current" pink task assignment(s).

Task assignment. A pink task assignment links to a yellow employee-as-skilled-one role (derivable). It also links to pink performance assessment(s).

Performance assessment. A pink performance assessment links to two yellow roles: employee as skilled one (derivable) and performance assessor.

Before and after. For position assignment, the preceding pink moment-intervals are project-activity detail (in project-activity management) and position-request detail.

Methods. Key methods include: make position assignment, make task assignment, make performance assessment, assess an employee's task workload, and compare assignments with skills.

Interactions. The "assess an employee's task workload" sequence is shown in Figure 4-9. A sender asks a yellow employee-as-skilled-one role to assess its task workload. It asks each of its pink current task assignments to get its hours per week. The employee-as-skilled-one role totals the hours and returns the result to the sender.

4.1.4 Work and Payment

Guided tour. The work-and-payment component is shown in Figure 4-10. The work-and-payment component has three moment-intervals, linked together: employee work, employee payment (two parts: payroll payment and expense payment), and pay period.

Employee work. A pink employee work links to a yellow employee-as-compensated-one role (derivable). It links to a green project account. It also links to pink payroll payment(s) and to pink expense payment(s).

Employee payment. Time for some inheritance here? After all, a payment could specialize into different kinds of payments. Yet how would we write that up? "Employee payment specializes into payroll payment and expense payment. A payment is one or the other, not both." Yet is that really true? Another, more flexible way to look at it is this: An employee payment may consist of payroll payments, expense payments, or both. Composition, rather than inheritance.

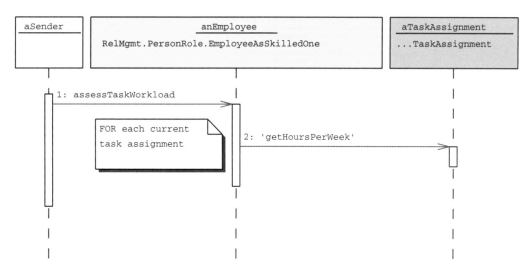

FIGURE 4-9. ▲ Assess an employee's task workload.

Tip. Transform inheritance (kinds of) into composition (parts of)? Nearly always, the result is more flexible. Do not use inheritance to factor out a common function (use composition and a plug-in point instead).

A pink employee payment links to a yellow person role, employee as compensated one (derivable link, via task assignment to "employee as skilled one" to person to "employee as compensated one"). It links to a yellow organization role, employer as compensation source.

An employee payment links to pink payroll payment(s) and to expense payment(s). An employee payment links to a green cost center. An employee payment also links to a pink pay period.

Pay period. A pink pay period captures the interval, accounting posting status, and employee payments for a pay period.

Before and after. For employee work, the preceding pink moment-interval is task assignment. The subsequent pink moment-interval is an accounting posting.

Methods. Key methods include: log employee work, make employee payment, calculate the total employee payments during a pay period (by cost center), and post payroll paid during a pay period (by cost center).

Interactions. The "post payroll paid by cost center" sequence is shown in Figure 4-11. A sender asks a pink pay period to post the payroll paid by cost center. The pay period does the work in two steps: First, calculate total; second, post.

In calculate total, a pink pay period asks each of its pink payroll payments for its amount and its cost center.

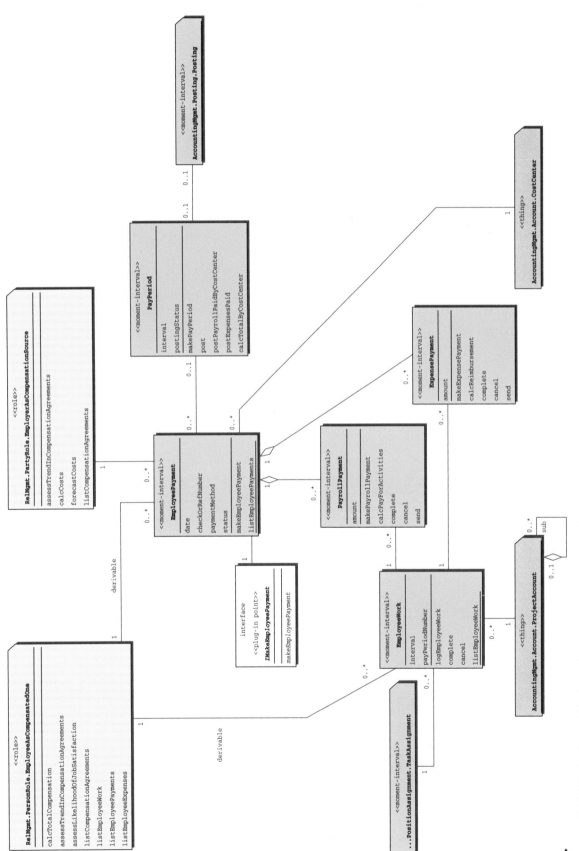

FIGURE 4-10. ▲ Work-and-payment component.

▲ 141

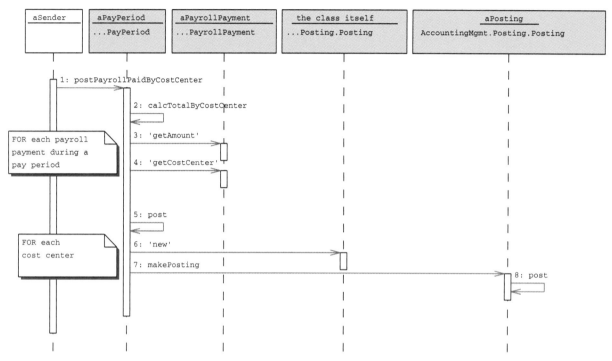

FIGURE 4-11. ▲ Post the payroll paid during pay period (by cost center).

In post, for each cost center, the pink pay period asks the pink posting class to create a new posting object, then asks that pink posting object to make a posting. The posting object posts the amount to that cost center's account.

4.1.5 Skill Acquisition

The skill-acquisition component captures employee skills and skill-building programs (workshops, seminars, on-the-job training, mentoring, and the like).

Guided tour. The skill-acquisition component is shown in Figure 4-12. The skill-acquisition component has a blue skill-acquisition program description and a trio of pink moment-intervals, linked together: skill-acquisition program, skill-acquisition program participation, and skill rating. For example:

Skill-acquisition program description	Java Modeling Workshop
Skill-acquisition program	The one starting next week
Skill-acquisition program participation	He participates in the workshop.
Skill rating, before and after	His skill rating, before and after

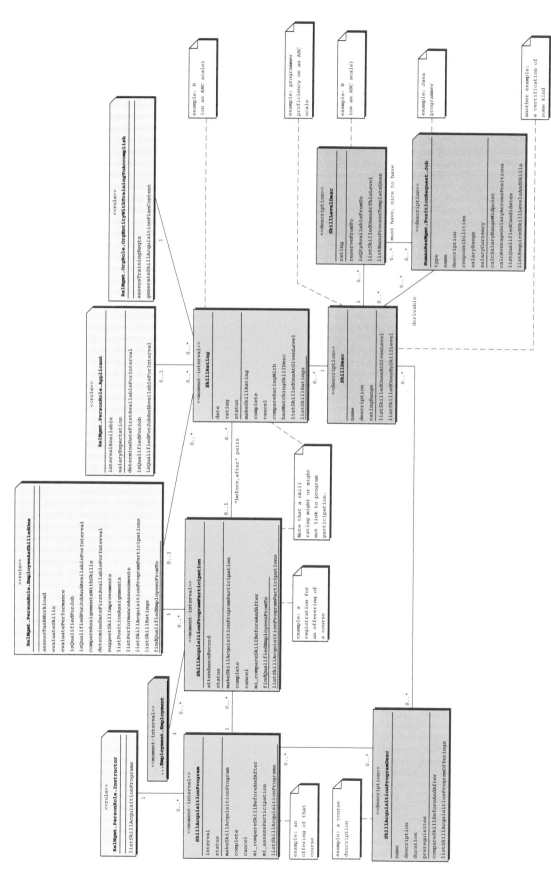

FIGURE 4-12. ▲ Skill-acquisition component.

Skill-acquisition program.   A pink skill-acquisition program links to a yellow instructor. It links to a blue skill-acquisition program description. It also links to pink skill-acquisition program participation(s).

Skill-acquisition program participation.   A pink skill-acquisition program participation links to a yellow employee-as-skilled-one role. It also links to pink skill ratings, organized into before and after pairs.

Before and after.   For skill-acquisition program participation, the preceding pink moment-interval is employment.

Methods.   Key methods include: make skill-acquisition program, make skill-acquisition program participation, make skill rating, is qualified for job, list skilled ones at a given level, and compare a skill (before and after).

Interactions.   The "compare a skill, before and after" sequence is shown in Figure 4-13. A sender asks its blue program description to compare a skill, before and after. The blue program description then asks each of its pink programs to compare a skill, before and after. Each program asks its pink program participations to compare a skill, before and after. A program participation iterates through its rating pairs, looking for the skill in question. Upon finding the right pair, a program participation asks the "after" object to compare itself with its "before" object. Program participation gets its difference. Program gets its collection of differences. Program description gets its collection of differences. And it returns the result to the sender.

4.2 RELATIONSHIP MANAGEMENT

What.   Relationship management spans persons, organizations, and the many roles that a person or organization might play.

Scope.   Relationship management spans party, party roles, person roles, and organization roles.

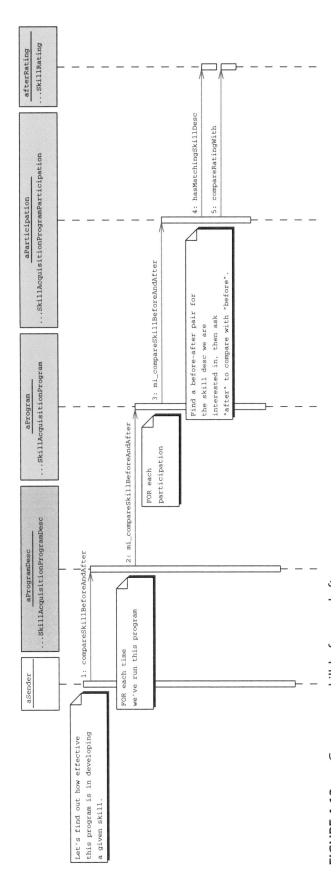

FIGURE 4-13. ▲ Compare a skill, before and after.

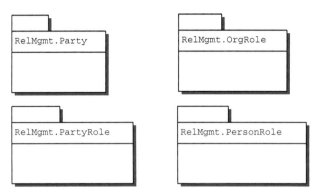

FIGURE 4-14. ▲ Relationship management components.

Links.   Relationship management is home for party and roles. As such, it links to all other components. In an implementation, one could package roles into usage groupings.

Components.   The components within relationship management are (Figure 4-14):

- Party
- Party role
- Person role
- Organization role

Moment-intervals.   The main moment-intervals for relationship management are:

- Party relationship
- Address use

Expansion.   One could expand this compound component by packaging roles into usage groupings.

4.2.1 Party

Guided tour.   The party component is shown in Figure 4-15. The party component has two pink moment-intervals, party relationship and address use. Yet it mainly revolves around a green party and a yellow party role.

Party relationship.   A pink party relationship links one or more green parties (persons or organizations) to one or more other parties (persons or organizations). A party relationship also links to a blue party-relationship description, establishing the kind of relationship.

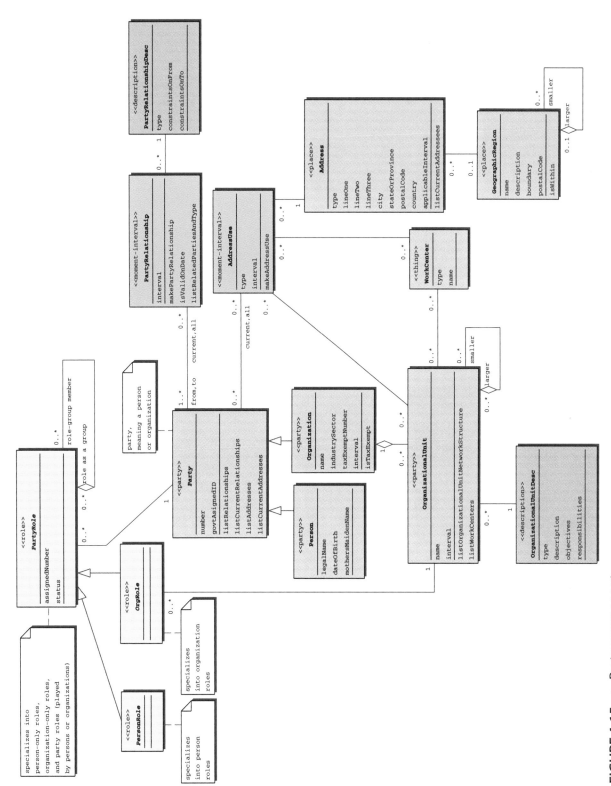

FIGURE 4-15. ▲ Party component.

Address use.   A pink address use links one or more parties (persons or organizations), organizational units, work centers, or some combination, to a green address, capturing both address-use type and applicable interval. A green address links to a green geographic region.

Party, person, and organization.   A party is a person or organization. This is stable problem-domain based generalization-specialization. Inheritance works well here. So a green party specializes into green person and organization. An organization links to some number of green organizational units.

Green organizational units link to larger and smaller organizational units, green work centers, and to a blue organizational-unit description (describing a category of organizational units).

A party links to a yellow party role. A person links to a yellow person role (person inherits the link defined in party). An organization links to a yellow organization role (organization inherits the link defined in party).

Party role.   The yellow party role is an abstract class (a class with no objects). It specializes into two abstract classes, person role and organization role. Each of these three classes specializes into respective role classes (presented in the components that follow).

Note that a party role might be a grouping of some number of other party roles. So an applicant might act as an applicant group, consisting of some number of other role-players.

Tip.   Groupings of roles or groupings of parties? Use groupings of roles rather than groupings of parties. This lets you work with groupings without affecting the parties involved. For example, an applicant group for a loan is just that: a group of applicants (a group of applicant-role objects, that is).

Methods.   Key methods include: make party relationship, make address use, list a party's current relationships, list a party's current addresses, and list an organizational unit's network structure.

Interactions.   The "list current relationships" sequence is shown in Figure 4-16. A sender asks a green party to list its current relationships. The party asks each of its pink current relationships to list the related parties and the relationship type.

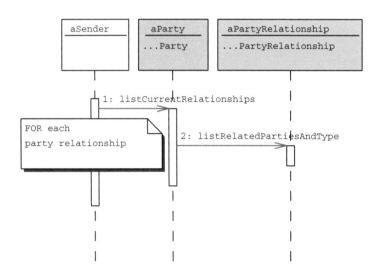

FIGURE 4-16. ▲ List current relationships.

4.2.2 Party Role

Guided tour.   The party-role component consists of yellow roles that people and organizations play. Party roles often appear in multiple components. So we organized them here, making it easier to find them and reuse them.

The party roles are shown in Figure 4-17. Note that each class is a specialization of party role. The diagram shows the inheritance links with text labels rather than with inheritance links, to avoid inheritance-link overload.

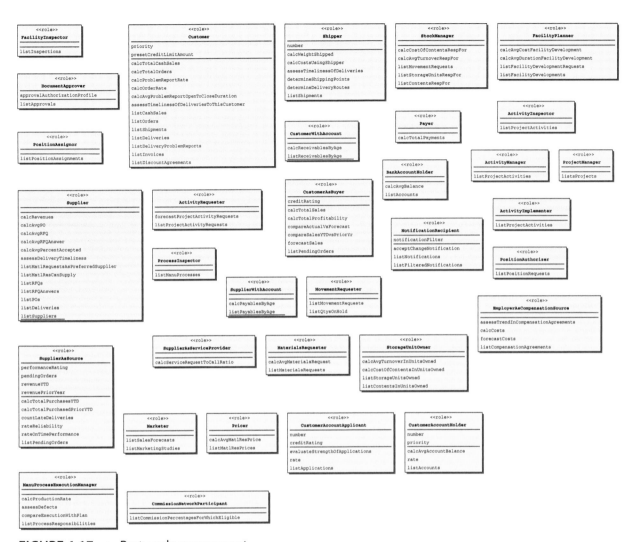

FIGURE 4-17. ▲ Party-role component.

4.2.3 Person Role

Guided tour.   The person-role component consists of yellow roles that people (not organizations) play. Person roles often appear in multiple components. So we organized them here, making it easier to find them and reuse them.

The person roles are shown in Figure 4-18. Note that each class is a specialization of person role. The diagram shows the inheritance links

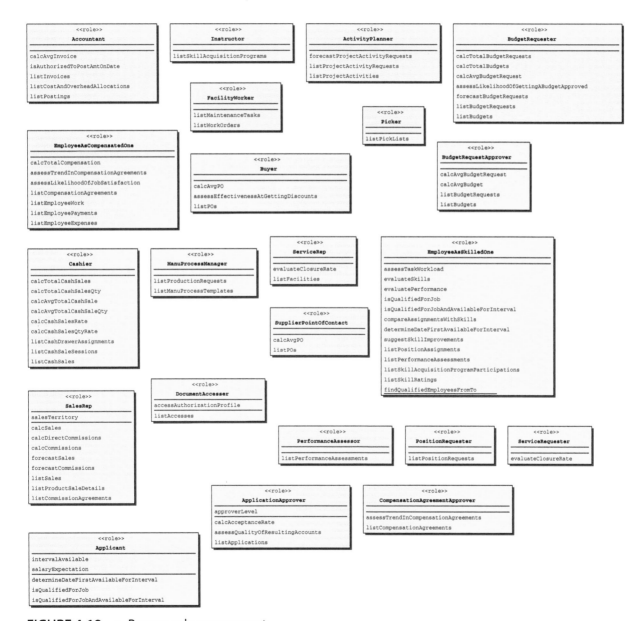

FIGURE 4-18. ▲ Person-role component.

with text labels rather than with inheritance links, to avoid inheritance-link overload.

4.2.4 Organization Role

Guided tour. The organization-role component consists of yellow roles that organizations (not people) play. Organization roles often appear in multiple components. So we organized them here, making it easier to find them and reuse them.

The organization roles are shown in Figure 4-19. Note that each class is a specialization of organization role. The diagram shows the inheritance links with text labels rather than with inheritance links, to avoid inheritance-link overload.

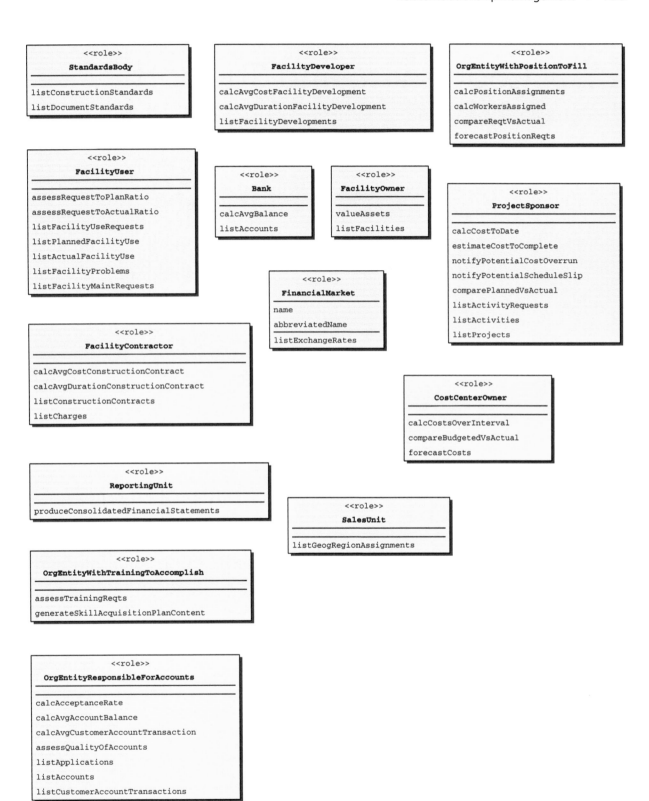

FIGURE 4-19. ▲ Organization-role component.

5 Coordinate and Support

▶ The example teaches.

A Latin proverb

This chapter presents three compound components:

1. Project-activity management
2. Accounting management
3. Document management

5.1 PROJECT-ACTIVITY MANAGEMENT

What. Project-activity management spans across all enterprise activities to be planned and executed. Project-activity management is the umbrella, the overall plan and execution, the one that activates smaller plans and executions within other components.

Scope. Project-activity management begins with a project and ends with activities.

Steps. First, establish a project. Second, make project-activity requests. Third, conduct activities. Fourth, use resource and activity pools to find workable combinations.

Links. Request material resources (material-resource management). Request manufacturing processes (manufacturing management). Request facility development (facility management). Request facility use (facility management), request inventory movement (inventory management), and request positions (human-resource management).

Components.   The components within project-activity management are (Figure 5-1):

- Project-activity request
- Project activity
- Activity-and-resource pool

Moment-intervals.   The pink moment-intervals for project-activity management are (Figure 5-2):

- Project
- Project-activity request
- Project activity

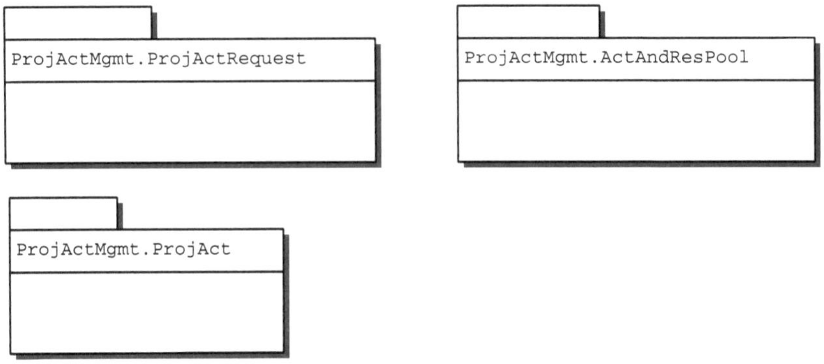

```
ProjActMgmt.ProjActRequest
```

```
ProjActMgmt.ActAndResPool
```

```
ProjActMgmt.ProjAct
```

FIGURE 5-1. ▲ Project-activity management components.

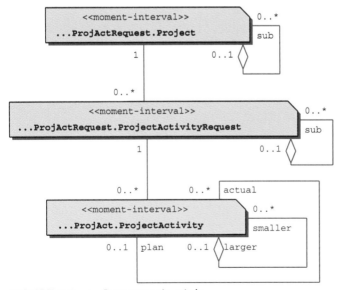

FIGURE 5-2. ▲ Summary in pink.

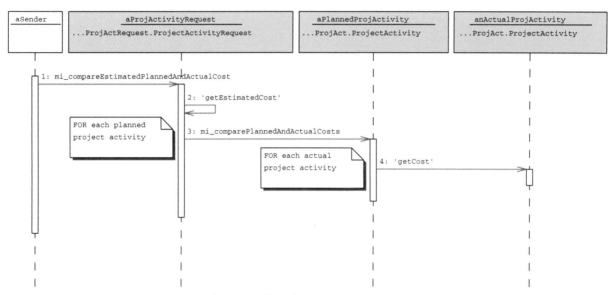

FIGURE 5-3. ▲ Compare estimated, planned, and actual cost.

Interactions.   The components work together to get things done. An example of inter-component interaction, "compare estimated, planned, and actual cost," is shown in Figure 5-3. A sender asks a pink project-activity request to compare its estimated, planned, and actual cost. It gets its estimated cost. It asks each of its pink planned project-activity objects to compare its planned and actual costs. Each planned project-activity object asks each of its actual project-activity objects to get its costs. Ultimately, the project-activity request returns a comparison of estimated, planned, and actual costs.

   Here's another example (Figure 5-4): A sender asks a pink project-activity request to estimate its percentage completion. The request ripples from project-activity request to each of its sub-requests (if any) to each of the corresponding project-request details and finally to component-specific requests. Ultimately, the project-activity request returns the result to the sender.

Expansion.   One could expand this compound component by adding planning coordination and planning simulation, plus work-breakdown structures and other planning tools.

5.1.1 Project-Activity Request

Guided tour.   The project-activity request component is shown in Figure 5-5. The project-activity request component has two pink moment-intervals, project and project-activity request.

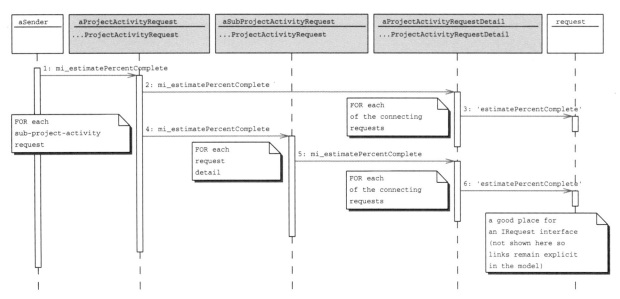

FIGURE 5-4. ▲ Estimate percent complete.

Project.   A pink project links to two yellow roles: project manager and project sponsor. It also links to a pink project-activity request.

Project-activity request.   A pink project-activity request links to two yellow roles: activity requester and activity planner. It links to a yellow organization-with-activity-to-accomplish role. It also links to pink project-activity request detail(s).

Project-activity request detail.   A pink project-activity request detail specifies interval and status, along with a link to one or more of the following:

- Materials request
- Production request
- Facility-development request
- Facility-use request
- Facility-maintenance request
- Movement request
- Position request

Activity-request pool.   A green activity-request pool is a collection of project-activity requests. It monitors those requests, selecting the next one; it asks that "next one" to generate a project activity.

Before and after.   For project-activity request, the subsequent pink moment-intervals are budget request and project activity. For

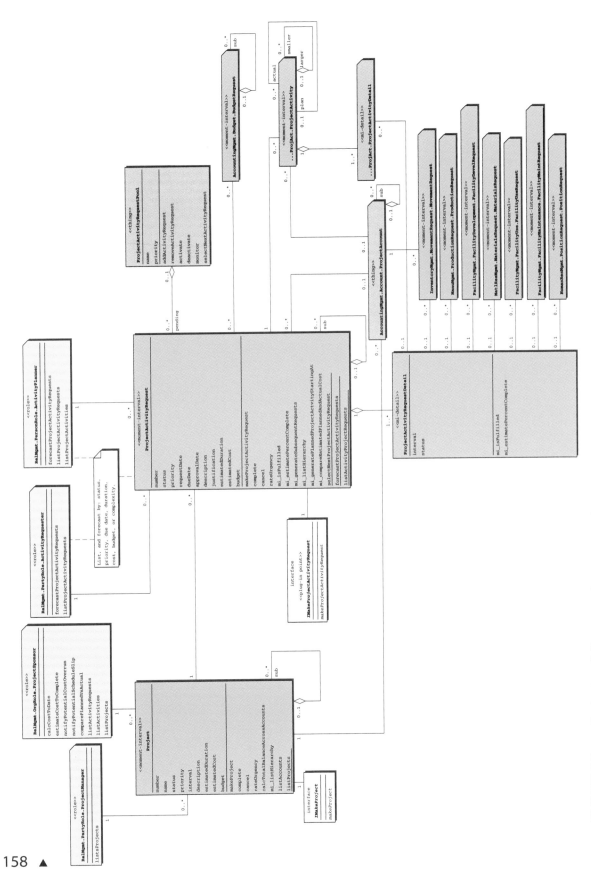

FIGURE 5-5. ▲ Project-activity request component.

project-activity request detail, the subsequent pink moment-interval details are project-activity detail, along with materials request (materials management), production request (manufacturing management), facility-development request (facility management), facility-use request (facility management), facility-maintenance request (facility management), movement request (inventory management), and position request (human-resource management).

Methods. Key methods include: make project-activity request, activate an activity pool, rate urgency, and generate project activity.

Interactions. The "activate an activity-request pool" sequence is shown in Figure 5-6. A sender asks a green activity-request pool to activate itself. The pool starts monitoring the requests in the pool. It selects the next project-activity request by asking each pink request to rate its urgency (for example, it might get its priority and get its due date). It selects the winning project-activity request and asks it to generate a corresponding project activity. The project-activity request sends a message to the project-activity class to create a new project-activity object, then asks that object to make a project activity, giving it the arguments it needs to do so.

Tip. Activate, deactivate, and monitor? Use activate/deactivate and monitor methods to express initial activation followed by some on-going behavior, running asynchronously over some period of time.

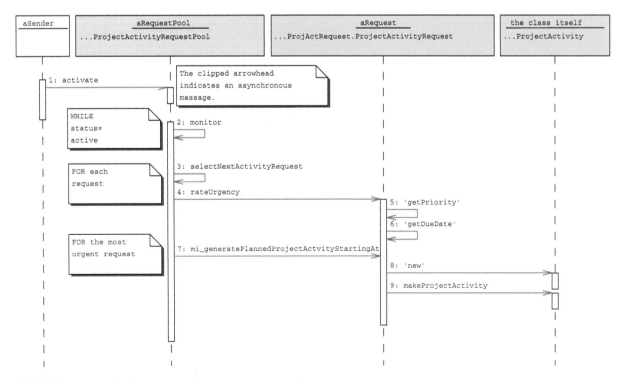

FIGURE 5-6. ▲ Activate an activity-request pool.

5.1.2 Project Activity

Guided tour. The project-activity component is shown in Figure 5-7. The project-activity component has one pink moment-interval, a project activity.

Project activity. A pink project activity links to a trio of yellow roles: activity manager, activity implementer, and activity inspector. It links to a green project account. It links to larger and smaller project activities. It also links to pink project-activity detail(s).

Also, a pink project activity links from a planned project activity to some number of actual executions of that project activity.

Tip. Plan then actual? Model with one class. Link each plan to actual(s). Label the link ends "plan 0..1" and "actual 0..*."

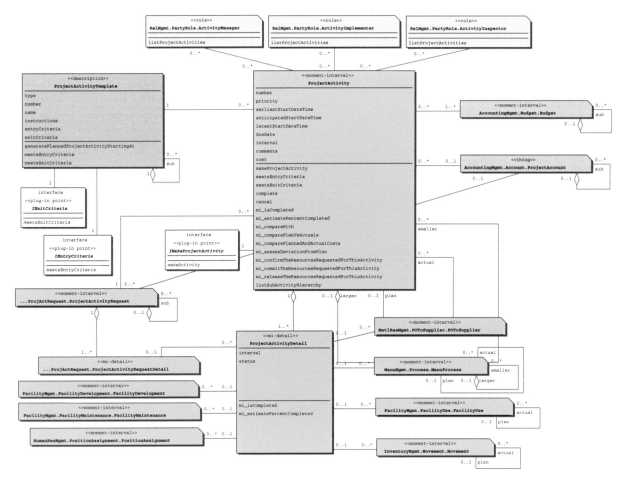

FIGURE 5-7. ▲ Project-activity component.

Project-activity detail. A pink project-activity detail specifies interval and status, along with a link to one or more of the following:

- PO to supplier
- Manufacturing process
- Facility development
- Facility use
- Facility maintenance
- Movement
- Position assignment

Before and after. For project activity, the preceding pink moment-intervals are project-activity request and budget. For project-activity detail, the preceding pink moment-interval detail is project-activity request detail. For project-activity detail, the subsequent pink moment-interval details are PO to supplier (materials management), manufacturing process (manufacturing management), facility use and facility maintenance (facility management), movement (inventory management), and position assignment (human-resource management).

Methods. Key methods include: make project activity, meets entry criteria, meets exit criteria, compare plan vs. actuals, and list sub-hierarchies.

Interactions. The "meets entry criteria" sequence is shown in Figure 5-8. A sender asks a pink project activity if it meets entry criteria. The project activity asks its blue project-activity template if the project activity meets the entry criteria. The template invokes its plug-in algorithm, asking it if it meets the entry criteria.

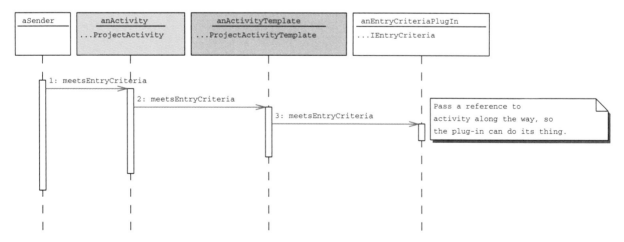

FIGURE 5-8. ▲ Meets entry criteria.

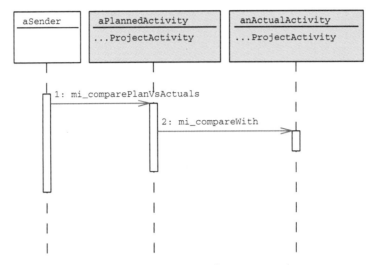

FIGURE 5-9. ▲ Compare plan vs. actuals.

The "compare plan vs. actuals" sequence is shown in Figure 5-9. A sender asks a pink planned project activity to compare the plan with its actuals. It in turn passes itself to each pink actual project activity, asking it to make a comparison. Ultimately, the result is returned to the sender.

The "list sub-hierarchies" sequence is shown in Figure 5-10. A sender asks a pink project activity to list its sub-activity hierarchy. It asks its pink

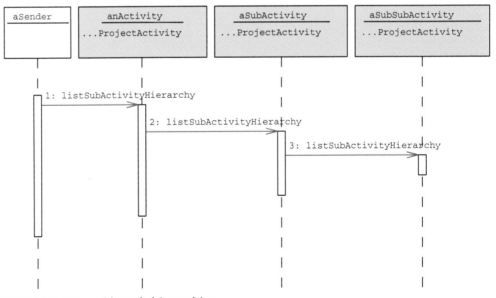

FIGURE 5-10. ▲ List sub-hierarchies.

project sub-activities to do the same. And so on. Ultimately, the result is returned to the sender.

5.1.3 Activity and Resource Pool

Guided tour.   The activity-and-resource pool component is shown in Figure 5-11. The activity-and-resource pool component consists of three key green pools: an activity pool, a resource pool, and an activity-and-resource pool.

All three pools encapsulate behavior across a collection. An activity pool tracks pending, in-progress, and blocked activities. It lists activities in "importance order." A resource pool tracks on-hold and in-use resources. It lists resources in "availability order." An activity-and-resource pool provides the operational research magic, finding activity and resource allocations that work.

Methods.   Key methods include: list planned project activities by priority, list resources by availability, and find project activity and resource allocations that work.

Interactions.   The "find activity-and-resource allocations that work" sequence is shown in Figure 5-12. A sender asks an overall pool to find activity and resource allocations that work. An overall pool asks each of its activity pools to list planned project activities by priority; it also asks each of its resource pools to list its resources by availability. Finally, an overall pool applies some operational-research management algorithms, to come up with a list of project activity and resource allocations that will work—and returns the result to the sender.

5.2 ACCOUNTING MANAGEMENT

What.   Accounting management tracks budgets, gathers accounting postings coming in from other components, and generates financial statements.

Scope.   Accounting management begins with accounts and ends with accounting postings for those accounts.

Steps.   First, define a chart of accounts (a list of accounts you use for tracking financial data). Second, establish accounts. Third, make budget requests. Fourth, establish budgets. Fifth, accept payments. Sixth, make accounting postings (officially record financial data).

Links.   Establish a budget request and budget for a project activity (from project-activity management). Establish a budget request and budget for facility development (to facility management). Accept accounting postings (from material-resource management, facility management, manufacturing management, inventory management, product sales, accounting management, and project-activity management).

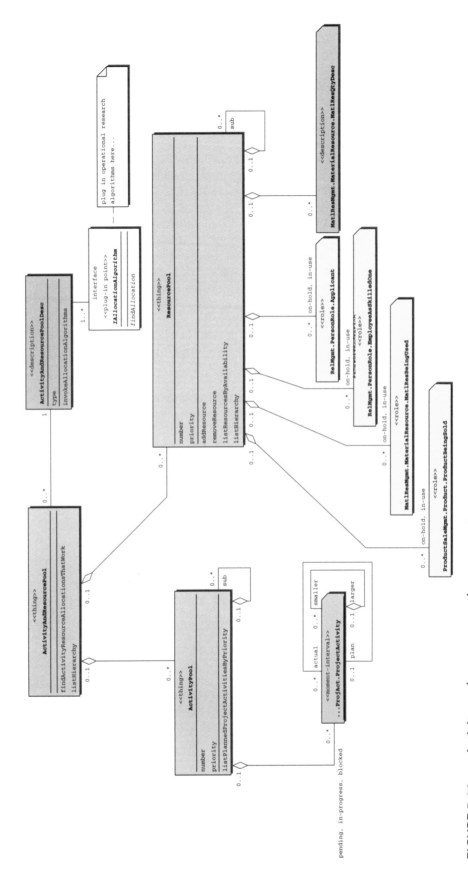

FIGURE 5-11. ▲ Activity-and-resource-pool component.

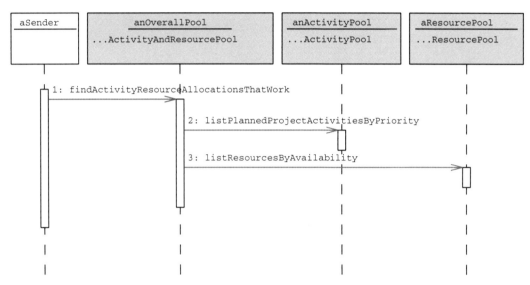

FIGURE 5-12. ▲ Find activity-and-resource allocations that work.

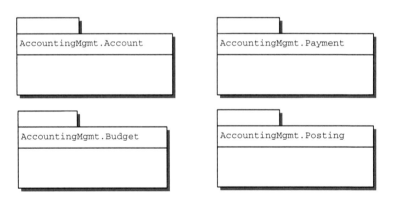

FIGURE 5-13. ▲ Accounting-management components.

Components. The components within accounting management are (Figure 5-13):

- Account
- Budget
- Payment
- Posting

Moment-intervals. The main moment-intervals for accounting management are (Figure 5-14):

- Budget request
- Budget
- Payment
- Posting

Interactions. The components work together to get things done. An example of inter-component interaction, "calculate credit postings," is shown in Figure 5-15. A sender asks a green account to calculate its credit postings. The account then iterates across its collection of postings, passing along the interval of interest as an argument. Each credit posting checks to make sure it's within the interval, then returns its amount (if within the interval) or zero (otherwise).

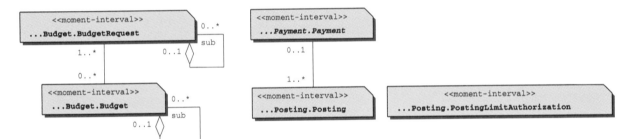

FIGURE 5-14. ▲ Summary in pink.

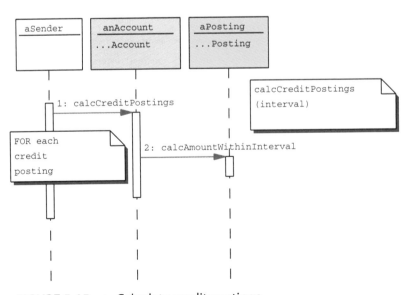

FIGURE 5-15. ▲ Calculate credit postings.

Expansion.   One could expand this compound component by enhancing the model with detailed account transactions and in-depth account analyses.

5.2.1 Account

The account component consists of the various accounts needed for accounting management.

Guided tour.   The account component is shown in Figure 5-16. The account component has a number of key green things: account, specializing into different kinds of accounts; general ledger; and cost center. It also tracks pink exchange rates for blue currency pair descriptions.

Account.   Account links to a blue account description. In addition, account specializes into different kinds of accounts. A green *general-ledger account* links to a green cost center and a green general ledger. A green *bank account* links to a yellow bank-account holder role and a yellow bank role. A green *project account* links to its sub-accounts and to a yellow project manager (via its project). The project account also links to its pink project and project activities. A green *customer account* links to its sub-accounts and to a yellow customer-with-account role. A green *supplier account* links to its sub-accounts and to a yellow supplier-with-account role.

General ledger.   A green general ledger is a collection of general-ledger accounts. It has a corresponding green chart of accounts. It also links to a yellow reporting-unit role.

Cost center.   A green cost center links to a green general-ledger account and to its yellow cost-center owner.

Exchange rate.   A pink exchange rate captures a buy and sell rate at a given point in time. It links to a blue currency-pair description. It also links to a yellow financial market.

Before and after.   For project account, the preceding moment-interval is project. For account, the subsequent pink moment-interval is budget detail.

Methods.   Key methods include: credit, debit, compare budgeted with actual, assess profitability from a general ledger.

Interactions.   The "assess profitability" sequence is shown in Figure 5-17. A sender asks a green general ledger to assess its profitability. The general ledger asks each of its green general-ledger accounts to get its balance and account type. The ledger adds up the results and returns the result to the sender.

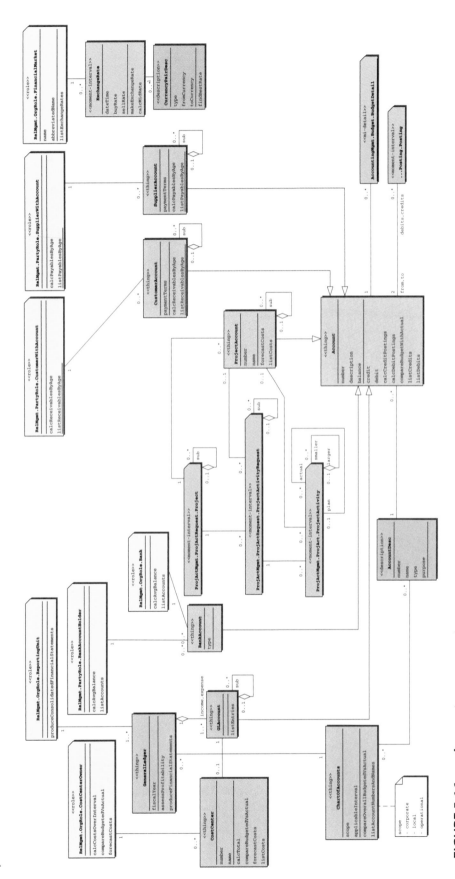

FIGURE 5-16. ▲ Account component.

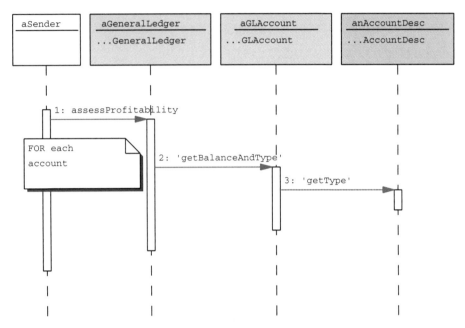

FIGURE 5-17. ▲ Assess profitability from a general ledger.

5.2.2 Budget

Guided tour. The budget component is shown in Figure 5-18. The budget component has two pink moment-intervals linked together: budget request and budget.

Budget request. A pink budget request links to two yellow roles: budget requester and budget approver. It also links to pink budget-request detail(s).

Budget-request detail. A pink budget-request detail specifies the amount requested and the amount approved. It also links to budget detail(s).

Look at the link between budget request and budget. A pink budget request might have some number of pink budgets.

Budget. A pink budget links to two yellow roles: budget requester and budget approver (both derivable). It also links to pink budget detail(s).

Budget detail. A pink budget detail specifies the amount requested and the amount approved. It also links back to a budget-request detail.

Before and after. For budget request, the preceding pink moment-interval is project-activity request. For budget, the subsequent pink moment-interval is project activity.

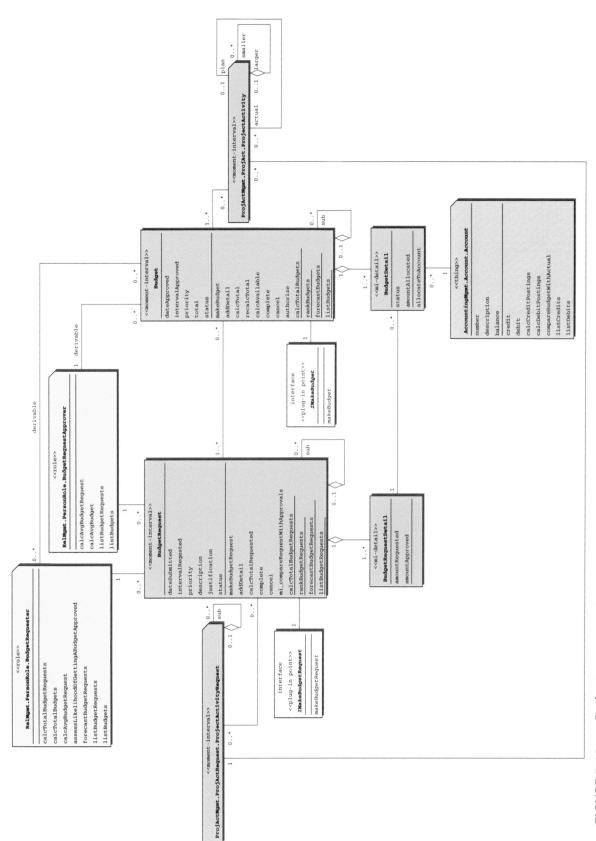

FIGURE 5-18. ▲ Budget component.

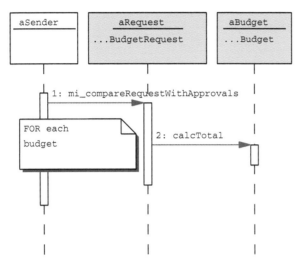

FIGURE 5-19. ▲ Compare budget request with approvals.

Methods.   Key methods include: make budget request, make budget, allocate budget detail to an account, and compare budget requests with approvals.

Interactions.   The "compare budget request with approvals" sequence is shown in Figure 5-19. A sender asks a pink request to compare itself with its subsequent approvals, meaning compare whether the entire request has been approved (a large request might require several incremental approvals). It asks each of its budgets to calculate its total.

5.2.3 Payment

Guided tour.   The payment component is shown in Figure 5-20. The payment component has one pink moment-interval, payment. A payment can come into the business (someone pays us) or go out from the business (we pay someone else).

Payment.   A pink payment links to a yellow payer. A payment comes in one of four flavors: check payment, cash payment, card payment, or electronic-funds transfer payment.

Pink check payment and card payment link to a green logical authorization system. It provides a layer of what we logically want to do with that authorization system: We ask it to authorize a payment. The logical authorization system links to a physical authorization-system proxy, a system-interaction class (shown in white) which in turn actually interacts with the other system.

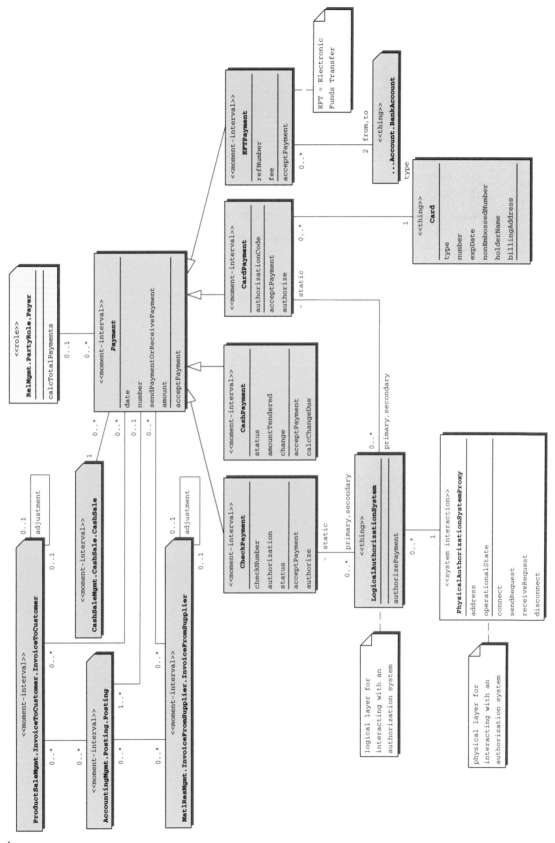

FIGURE 5-20. ▲ Payment component.

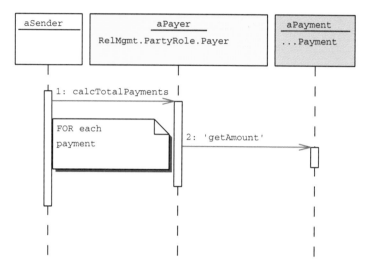

FIGURE 5-21. ▲ Calculate total payments made by a payer.

Before and after.   For payment, the preceding pink moment-intervals are invoice to customer, cash sale, and invoice from supplier. The subsequent pink moment-interval is an accounting posting.

Methods.   Key methods include: accept payment, authorize payment, calculate change due, and calculate total payment made by a payer.

Interactions.   The "calculate total payments made by a payer" sequence is shown in Figure 5-21. A sender asks a yellow payer to calculate its total payments. It asks each of its payments for its amounts, totals the amounts, and returns the result to the sender.

5.2.4 Posting

Guided tour.   The posting component is shown in Figure 5-22. The posting component has two pink moment-intervals: posting-limit authorization and posting.

Posting-limit authorization.   A pink posting-limit authorization links to a yellow accountant role.

Posting.   A pink posting links to a yellow accountant role. It links to a blue posting description, describing the posting category. And it links to a "from" account and a "to" account.

Before and after.   For posting, the preceding pink moment-interval is a resource-consuming pink moment-interval (in another component).

Methods.   Key methods include: "is authorized to post amount on date" and make a posting.

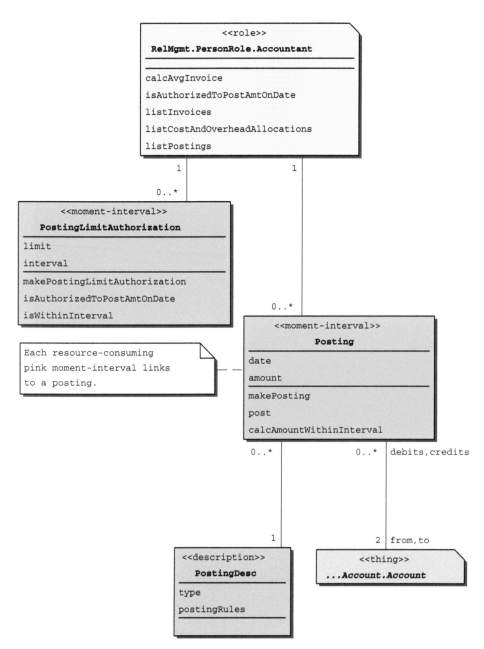

FIGURE 5-22. ▲ Posting component.

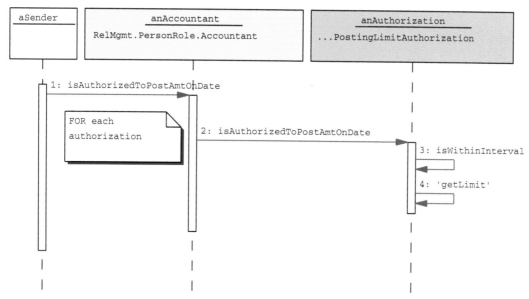

FIGURE 5-23. ▲ Is authorized to post amount on date.

Interactions. The "is authorized to post amount on date" sequence is shown in Figure 5-23. A sender asks a yellow accountant if it is authorized to post an amount on a specific date. The accountant asks each of its authorizations if it provides the needed authorization. An authorization checks if the date is within its applicable interval, gets its limits, determines whether or not it is authorized, and returns the result to accountant. Once done, the accountant object returns the result to the sender.

5.3 DOCUMENT MANAGEMENT

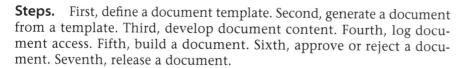

What. Document and record research results, business results, and legal dealings.

Scope. Document management begins with document templates and ends with document releases.

Steps. First, define a document template. Second, generate a document from a template. Third, develop document content. Fourth, log document access. Fifth, build a document. Sixth, approve or reject a document. Seventh, release a document.

Components. The components within document management are (Figure 5-24):

- Document
- Document activity

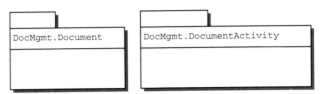

FIGURE 5-24. ▲ Document-management components.

Interactions. The components work together to get things done. An example of inter-component interaction, "build document in XML," is shown in Figure 5-25. A sender asks a green document to build an XML document. A document asks each of its parts to build an XML document (that part of the overall document). After that, a document asks the document-build class to create an object; then it sends a "make document build" message, to save the build and capture information about it.

Expansion. One could expand this component with document storage and document traceability.

5.3.1 Document

Guided tour. The document component is shown in Figure 5-26. The document component consists of blue document templates, followed by green documents.

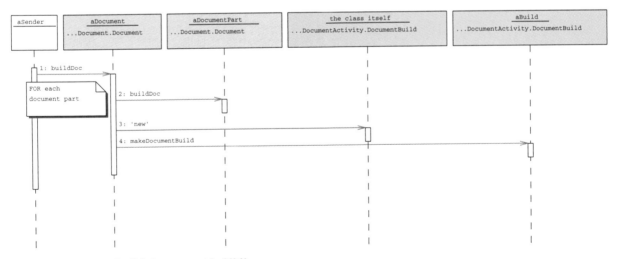

FIGURE 5-25. ▲ Build document in XML.

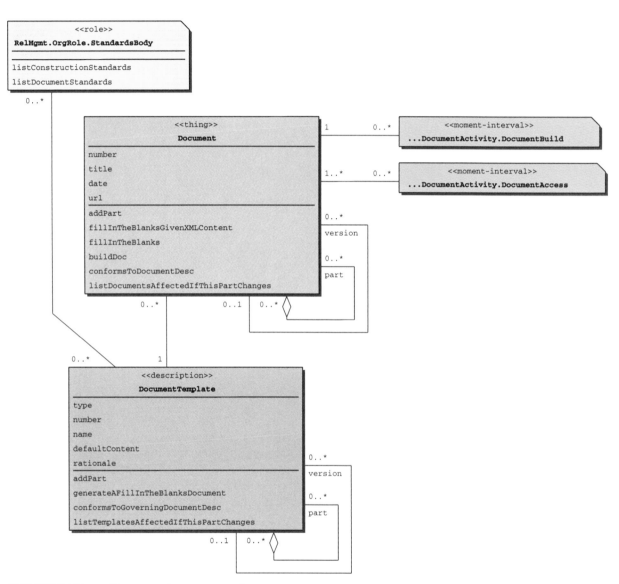

FIGURE 5-26. ▲ Document component.

Document template.   A blue document template links to versions. It also consists of some number of parts.

Document.   A green document links to versions. It also consists of some number of parts.

Methods.   Key methods include: generate a fill-in-the-blanks document, fill in the blanks given XML content, build a document, and list documents affected if this part changes.

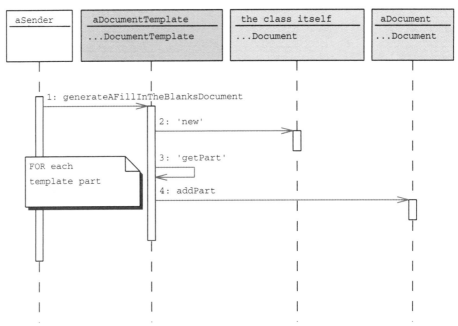

FIGURE 5-27. ▲ Generate a fill-in-the-blanks document.

Interactions. The "generate a fill-in-the-blanks document" sequence is shown in Figure 5-27. A sender asks a blue document template to generate a fill-in-the-blanks document. The template sends a message to the document class, to create a document. Then the template gets template parts and asks the document to add document parts.

The "fill in the blanks given XML content" sequence is shown in Figure 5-28. A sender asks a green document to fill in the blanks, given XML content. It fills in its own blanks. And it asks its document parts to fill in its blanks, too.

5.3.2 Document Activity

Guided tour. The document-activity component is shown in Figure 5-29. The document-activity component has four pink moment-intervals, linked together: document build, document approval, document release, and document access.

These four moment-intervals track the progression from a build to some number of approvals to some number of releases to some number of document accesses. If for a build there is always just one approval and just one release, then the three subsequent moments in time can be more simply modeled as attributes within the build class (date built, date approved, date rejected, and date released).

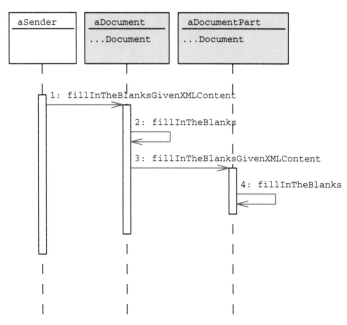

FIGURE 5-28. ▲ Fill in the blanks given XML content.

A pink document approval links to a yellow document approver. A pink document access links to a yellow document accesser and to a green document.

Tip. A pink moment-interval object with at most one corresponding subsequent moment-interval object? Consider merging the two, resulting in a simpler overall model.

Methods. Key methods include: make document access/build/approval/ release, and generate document approval/release.

Interactions. The "generate document release" sequence is shown in Figure 5-30. A sender asks a pink document approval to generate a document release. It asks the document release class to create an object. Then it sends a message to that object, asking it to make a document release.

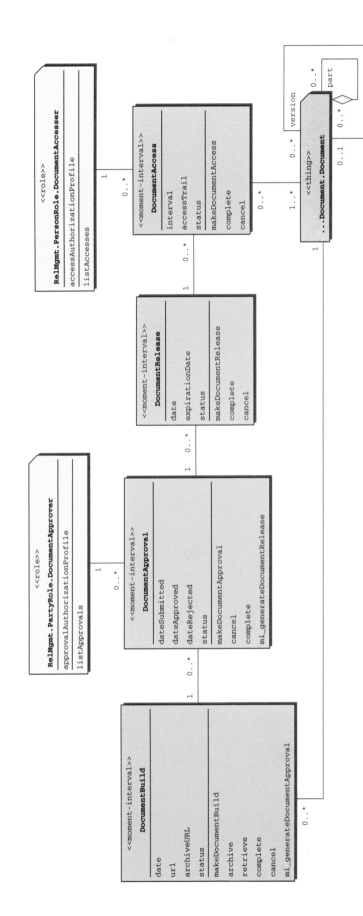

FIGURE 5-29. ▲ Document-activity component.

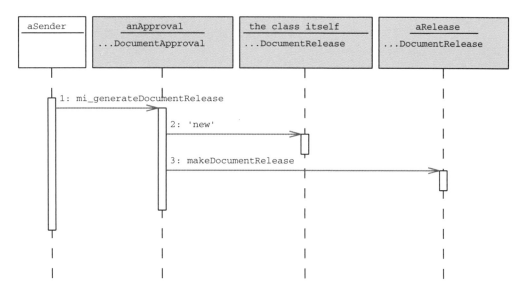

FIGURE 5-30. ▲ Generate document release.

6

Feature-Driven Development

> ▶ I feel a recipe is only a theme which an intelligent cook can play each time with a variation.
>
> *Madame Benoit*

> ▶ The ultimate judgment of progress is this: measurable results in reasonable time.
>
> *Robert Anthony*

> ▶ I measure output, not input.
>
> *Lim Bak Wee*

For enterprise-component modeling to be successful, it must live and breathe within a larger context, a software development process.

We've developed such a process in practice, and we detail it in this chapter. We present Feature-Driven Development (FDD) in these sections:

1. The problem: accommodating shorter and shorter business cycles
2. The solution: feature-driven development
3. Defining feature sets and features
4. Establishing a process: why and how
5. The five processes within FDD
6. Chief programmers, class owners, and feature teams
7. Management controls: Tracking progress with precision

6.1 THE PROBLEM: ACCOMMODATING SHORTER AND SHORTER BUSINESS CYCLES

Despite the many advances in software development, it is not uncommon for projects lasting two or more years to use a function-driven process: from functional specs (in traditional paragraph format or in use-case format) to design to code to test to deployment. Along the way, some have made minor modifications to the theme, allowing some influence from iterations. Nevertheless, many software projects exceed budget, blow schedule, and deliver something less than desired (something appropriate two years earlier, yet no longer).

As if that weren't enough pressure, the ever-increasing pace of technological advances makes it less and less likely that a project lasting more than two years will ever succeed.

In fact, more and more, we are mentoring projects with total schedules of 90, 120, or 180 days—or perhaps 9, 12, or 18 months. One market-leader we work with considers any project longer than 180 days as high-risk. Why? Their business changes so rapidly and the supporting technology changes so rapidly that planning nine months out adds risk to the project.

That's quite a change in perspective.

The authors of *BLUR: The Speed of Change in the Connected Economy* put it this way:

> Speed is the foreshortening of product life cycles from years to months or even weeks. . . . Accelerated product life cycles and time-based competition have become part of the business lingo. . . . The faster things move, the less time you have to plan for them. You're much better off iterating and reiterating, adjusting as you go.
>
> STAN DAVIS AND CHRISTOPHER MEYER [DAVIS98]

The norm for fast-cycle-time projects is a feature-driven iterative process, beginning with features and modeling, followed by design-and-build increments.

In this chapter, we formalize the process we call "Feature-Driven Development" (FDD).

We've developed FDD in practice. Project teams apply it with significant success.

Developers like it. With FDD, they get something new to work on every two weeks. (Developers love new things.) With FDD, they get closure every two weeks. Closure is an important must-have element for job satisfaction. Getting to declare "I'm done" every two weeks is such a good thing.

Managers like it too. With FDD, they know what to plan and how to establish meaningful milestones. They get the risk-reduction that comes from managing a project that delivers frequent, tangible, working results. With FDD, they get real percentage numbers on progress, for example, being 57% complete and demonstrating to clients and to senior management exactly where the project is.

Clients like it too. With FDD, they see plans with milestones that they understand. They see frequent results that they understand. And they know exactly how far along the project is at any point in time.

Yes, developers *and* managers *and* clients like FDD. Amazing yet true.

6.2 THE SOLUTION: FEATURE-DRIVEN DEVELOPMENT

What if you and your team adopted a process for delivering frequent, tangible, working results?

Think about it. You could plan for results, measure results, measure your progress in a believable way, and demonstrate working results.

What might this mean for you and your career, the morale of your team, and added business from your clients? Plenty of motivation!

FDD is a model-driven short-iteration process. It begins with establishing an overall model shape. Then it continues with a series of two-week "design by feature, build by feature" iterations.

The features are small "useful in the eyes of the client" results.

Most iterative processes are anything but short and "useful in the eyes of the client." An iteration like "build the accounting subsystem" would take too long to complete. An iteration like "build the persistence layer" is not (directly at least) client-valued.

Moreover, long and IT-centric iterations make life difficult. It's harder to track what's really going on during an iteration. And it's harder to engage the client, not having a steady stream of client-valued results to demonstrate along the way.

In contrast, a small feature like "assign unique order number" is both short and client-valued. In fact, a client knows exactly what it is, can assign a priority to it, can talk about what is needed, and can assess whether or not it truly meets the business need.

A small feature is a tiny building block for planning, reporting, and tracking. It's understandable. It's measurable. It's do-able (with several other features) within a two-week increment.

As in any other development process, FDD prescribes a series of steps and sub-steps. Unlike other processes, FDD uniquely:

- uses very small blocks of client-valued functionality, called features (allowing users to describe what they want in short statements, rather than having to force those thoughts into a "the user does this, the system does that" format),
- organizes those little blocks into business-related groupings (solving the dilemma of what level one should write use-cases for),

- focuses developers on producing working results every two weeks,
- facilitates inspections (making inspections, a best practice, easier to accept and simpler to apply),
- provides detailed planning and measurement guidance,
- promotes concurrent development within each "design by feature, build by feature" increment,
- tracks and reports progress with surprising accuracy, and
- supports both detailed tracking within a project and higher-level summaries for higher-level clients and management, in business terms.

6.3 DEFINING FEATURE SETS AND FEATURES

A *feature* is a client-valued function that can be implemented in two weeks or less.

We name a feature using this template:

<action> the <result> <by|for|of|to> a(n) <object>

where an object is a person, place, or thing (including roles, moments in time or intervals of time, or catalog-entry-like descriptions)

For example,

- Calculate the total of a sale.
- Assess the fulfillment timeliness of a sale.
- Calculate the total purchases by a customer.

A *feature set* is a grouping of business-related features. We name a feature set this way:

<action><-ing> a(n) <object>

An example is "making a product sale."

And we name a major feature set this way:

<object> management

An example is "product-sales management."

We start an informal features list while developing the overall model. We write down features we hear from domain members and glean content from documents we are working with.

We build a detailed features list after developing an overall model. Some features come by transforming methods in the model to features. Most features come from considering each pink moment-interval (business areas) and writing down the features.

For example, see the model snippet in Figure 6-1.

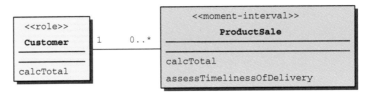

FIGURE 6-1. ▲ A model snippet.

We could transform its methods into:

- Feature set
    Making a product sale to a customer
- Features
    Calculate the total of a sale.
    Assess fulfillment timeliness for a sale.
    Calculate the total purchases by a customer.

Yet we can do even more, considering additional features that will better satisfy client wants and needs. Here's an example:

- Major feature set
    Product-sale management
- Feature set
    Making a product sale to a customer
- Features
    Calculate the total of a sale.
    Assess the fulfillment timeliness for a sale.
    Calculate the total purchases by a customer.
    Calculate the tax for a sale.
    Assess the current preferences of a customer.

For each additional feature, we add corresponding methods to the model. Normally we don't do this right away, but rather during the "design by feature, build by feature" iterations.

In practice, we've seen again and again that building an overall model and an informal features list before developing a detailed features list:

- brings domain members together to talk with each other, listen to each other, and develop a common model of the business—before developing a fully detailed features list,

- increases developer members' understanding about the domain and how things interrelate within it (even if they have built systems in the domain before),

- fosters more creativity and innovation (visual models in color engage spatial thinking, a creativity must-have before moving into linguistic and mathematical-logical thinking),
- encourages exploring "what could be done, what might be done, and what could make a real difference" before locking oneself into a fixed system boundary ("the user does this, the system does that"), and
- leads to the discovery of feature sets and features that bring significant business advantage, rather than passively scribing down the needs for yet another system.

6.4 ESTABLISHING A PROCESS: WHY AND HOW

This section explores these questions:

1. Why use a process?
2. Who selects tools for a process?
3. How might one describe a process?

6.4.1 Why Use a Process?

We think most process initiatives are silly. Well-intentioned managers and teams get so wrapped up in executing process that they forget that they are being paid for results, not process execution.

Process for process' sake alone, as a matter of "process pride," is a shame. Having hundreds of pages of steps to execute demoralizes the team members, to the point that they willingly turn off their minds and simply follow the steps.

Process over-specification does far more harm than good. The process takes on a life of its own and consumes more and more time that could be otherwise spent actually developing software.

A decade ago, one of us wrote up a 110-page process for a large development team. No matter how hard he tried to defend every word of his process as something of great value, the team members looked at the four-page summary in the back and ignored the rest of what he thought was valuable content. He learned from that experience: No matter how much process pride you might have as a leader, short one- to two-page process guides are what developers really want and need.

No amount of process over-specification will make up for bad people. Far better: Staff your project with good people, do whatever it takes to keep them happy, and use simple, well-bounded processes to guide them along the way.

A well-defined and (relatively speaking) lightweight process can help your team members work together to achieve remarkable and noteworthy results. This is significant and worthy of additional consideration.

In this light then, let's take a look at the top reasons for developing and using a process:

1. Move to larger projects and repeatable success.
2. Bring new staff in with a shorter ramp-up time.
3. Focus on high-payoff results.

6.4.1.1 Move to larger projects and repeatable success.

To move to larger projects and repeatable success, you need a good process, a system for building systems.

Simple, well-defined processes work best. Team members apply them several times, make refinements, and commit the process to memory. It becomes second nature to them. It becomes a good habit.

Good habits are a wonderful thing. They allow the team to carry out the basic steps, focusing on content and results, rather than process steps. This is best achieved when the process steps are logical and their worth immediately obvious to each team member.

With complex processes, about all you can hope for is "process pride," since learning and applying the process can keep you away from getting the real work accomplished.

With good habits in using simple, well-defined processes, the process itself moves from foreground to background. Team members focus on results rather than process micro-steps. Progress accelerates. The team reaches a new stride. The team performs!

6.4.1.2 Bring new staff in with a shorter ramp-up time.

Well bounded, simple processes allow the easy introduction of new staff: it dramatically shortens their learning curves and reduces the time it takes to become effective and efficient. When there is a practiced and simple system in place, it takes far less time for someone new to understand how things are done and to become effective. Standardization benefits also come into play here if processes are subject to them (standard language, process templates, naming conventions, where to find things, and the like).

It is far more effective to be able to spend a little time on process training and a lot of time on problem-domain training. The ramp-up to being productive will be shorter and much more efficient.

6.4.1.3 Focus on high-payoff results.

We've seen far too many technologists going beyond what is needed, and in extreme cases striving for (unattainable) perfection on one part of a project, without considering the other parts they compromise by doing so.

It's absolutely essential that your team focuses and stays focused on producing high-payoff results. Here are some suggestions for doing just that.

Help the team come to grips with this proverb:

> Every time you choose to do, you choose to leave something else undone. Choose wisely.

Peter Coad Sr.

That means (in this context) setting and keeping priorities, building the must-have features, getting to "good enough," and not going beyond till other features get their due.

Make weekly progress reports visible to everyone on the team. And make individual progress visible at each desk. Here's how: Use your own form of "features completed on time" scorecards. Some organizations use colorful stickers for this, indicating "feature kills" (features completed on time) and "feature misses" (features that are late). The politically correct prefer "feature wins" rather than "feature kills."

6.4.2 Who Selects Tools for a Process?

Across-the-team-uniformity of tools in dealing with the various process artifacts streamlines what you do. So project tool selection is another important area to have well bounded.

Yet who selects tools? And who builds them?

We find that it's a good idea to designate a Tools Board, one or more people with the charter of defining tools to support the process, selecting most tools from vendors, and building smaller in-house tools as needed.

Use the Tools Board to drive all tooling decisions. And use its existence to thwart side-tracks by your best and brightest (who might occasionally fall in love with a custom tool and spend valuable time designing and building that tool, rather than designing and building client-valued project results).

But beware: Tools for the sake of tools is just as bad as process for the sake of process. Tools support the process. The Tool Board should strive to ensure that the tools work well together in a team environment. If a tool gets in the way, get rid of it. Tools are a means to an end.

6.4.3 How Might One Describe a Process?

The best processes we've applied were expressed in one or two pages. Surprised? It takes extra effort to write a process with simplicity, clarity, and brevity. As Pascal once put it:

> I have made this letter longer than usual, because I lack the time to make it short.[1]

BLAISE PASCAL

---

[1]"Je n'ai fait cette lettre plus longue que parce que je n'ai pas eu le loisir de la faire plus courte." Blaise Pascal, *Lettres Provinciales* (1656–1657), no. 4.

The best pattern we've found for writing process templates is called ETVX: Entry, Task, Verification, and eXit:

1. Specify clear and well defined entry criteria for the process (can't start without these precursors).

2. Then list the tasks for that process with each task having a title, the project roles that participate in that task, whether that task is optional or required, and a task description (what am I to be doing?).

3. Next, specify the means of verification for the process (when have I accomplished "good enough" functionality?).

4. Finally, specify the exit criteria for the process, that is, how you know when you are complete and what the outputs (work products) are.

Clearly defined process tasks allow you to progress more efficiently. Without them, each developer makes his own way and ends up working harder than necessary to get the desired results.

Exit criteria must define tangible outputs. Define what the produced work products are, what the format is, and where the results go.

6.5 THE FIVE PROCESSES WITHIN FDD

This section presents the five processes within FDD (Figure 6-2):

- Process #1: Develop an overall model (using initial requirements/ features, snap together with components, focusing on shape).
- Process #2: Build a detailed, prioritized features list.
- Process #3: Plan by feature.
- Process #4: Design by feature (using components, focusing on sequences).
- Process #5: Build by feature.

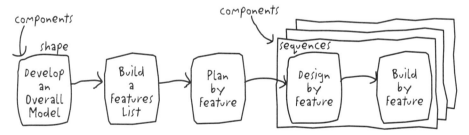

FIGURE 6-2. ▲ The five processes within FDD.

FDD Process #1: Develop an Overall Model

Domain and development members, under the guidance of an experienced component/object modeler (chief architect), work together in this process. Domain members present an initial high-level, highlights-only walk-through of the scope of the system and its context. The domain and development members produce a skeletal model, the very beginnings of that which is to follow. Then the domain members present more detailed walkthroughs. Each time, the domain and development members work in small sub-teams (with guidance from the chief architect); present sub-team results; merge the results into a common model (again with guidance from the chief architect), adjusting model shape along the way.

In subsequent iterations of this process, smaller teams tackle specialized domain topics. Domain members participate in many yet not all of those follow-up sessions.

Entry Criteria

The client is ready to proceed with the building of a system. He might have a list of requirements in some form. Yet he is not likely to have come to grips with what he really needs and what things are truly "must have" vs. "nice to have." And that's okay.

Tasks

Form the Modeling Team	Project Management	Required

The modeling team consists of permanent members from both domain and development areas. Rotate other project staff through the modeling sessions so that everyone gets a chance to observe and participate.

Domain Walkthrough	Modeling Team	Required

A domain member gives a short tutorial on the area to be modeled (from 20 minutes to several hours, depending upon the topic). The tutorial includes domain content that is relevant to the topic yet a bit broader than the likely system scope.

Study Documents	Modeling Team	Optional

The team scours available documents, including (if present): component models, functional requirements (traditional or use-case format), data models, and user guides.

Build an Informal Features List	Chief Architect, Chief Programmers	Required

The team builds an informal features list, early work leading up to FDD Process #2. The team notes specific references (document and page number) from available documents, as needed.

Develop Sub-team Models	Modeling Team in Small Groups	Required

The Chief Architect may propose a component or suggest a starting point. Using archetypes (in color) and components, each sub-team builds a class diagram for the domain under consideration, focusing on classes and links, then methods, and finally attributes. The sub-teams add methods from domain understanding, the initial features list, and methods suggested by the archetypes. The sub-teams sketch one or more informal sequence diagrams, too.

Develop a Team Model	Chief Architect, Modeling Team	Required

Each sub-team presents its proposed model for the domain area. The chief architect may also propose an additional alternative. The modeling team selects one of the proposed models as a baseline, merges in content from the other models, and keeps an informal sequence diagram. The team updates its overall model. The team annotates the model with notes, clarifying terminology and explaining key model-shape issues.

Log Alternatives	Chief Architect, Chief Programmers	Required

A team scribe (a role assigned on a rotating basis) logs notes on significant modeling alternatives that the team evaluated, for future reference on the project.

Verification

Internal and External Assessment	Modeling Team	Required

Domain members, active in the process, provide internal self-assessment. External assessment is made on an as-needed basis, to clarify domain understanding, functionality needs, and scope.

Exit Criteria

To exit this process, the team must deliver the following results, subject to review and approval by the development manager and the chief architect:
- Class diagrams with (in order of descending importance) classes, links, methods, and attributes. Classes and links establish model shape. Methods (along with the initial features list and informal sequence diagrams) express functionality and are the raw materials for building a features list. Plus informal sequence diagrams.
- Informal features list
- Notes on significant modeling alternatives

FDD Process #2: Build a Features List

The team identifies the features, groups them hierarchically, prioritizes them, and weights them.

In subsequent iterations of this process, smaller teams tackle specialized feature areas. Domain members participate in many yet not all of those follow-up sessions.

Entry Criteria
The modeling team has successfully completed FDD Process #1, Develop an Overall Model.

Tasks

Form the Features-List Team	Project Manager, Development Manager	Required

The features-list team consists of permanent members from the domain and development areas.

Identify Features, Form Feature Sets	Features-List Team	Required

The team begins with the informal features list from FDD Process #1. It then:
- transforms methods in the model into features,
- transforms moment-intervals in the model into feature sets (and groupings of moment-intervals into major feature sets),
- (and mainly it) Brainstorms, selects, and adds features that will better satisfy client wants and needs.

It uses these formats:
- For features: <action> the <result> <by|for|of|to> a(n) <object>
- For feature sets: <action><-ing> a(n) <object>
- For major feature sets: <object> management

where an object is a person, place, or thing (including roles, moments in time or intervals of time, or catalog-entry-like descriptions)

Prioritize the Feature Sets and Features	Features-List Team	Required

A subset of the team, the Features Board establishes priorities for feature sets and features. Priorities are A (must have), B (nice to have), C (add it if we can), or D (future). In setting priorities, the team considers each feature in terms of client satisfaction (if we include the feature) and client dissatisfaction (if we don't).

Divide Complex Features	Features-List Team	Required

The development members, led by the chief architect, look for features that are likely to take more than two weeks to complete. The team divides those features into smaller features (steps).

Verification

Internal and External Assessment	Features-List Team	Required

Domain members, active in the process, provide internal self-assessment. External assessment is made on an as-needed basis, to clarify domain understanding, functionality needs, and scope.

Exit Criteria
To exit this process, the features-list team must deliver a detailed features list, grouped into major feature sets and feature sets, subject to review and approval by the development manager and the chief architect.

FDD Process #3: Plan by Feature

Using the hierarchical, prioritized, weighted features list, the project manager, the development manager, and the chief programmers establish milestones for "design by feature, build by feature" iterations.

Entry Criteria

The features-list team has successfully completed FDD Process #2, Build a Features List.

Tasks

Form the Planning Team	Project Manager	Required

The planning team consists of the project manager, the development manager, and the chief programmers.

Sequence Major Feature Sets and Features	Planning Team	Required

The planning team determines the development sequence and sets initial completion dates for each feature set and major feature set.

Assign Classes to Class Owners	Planning Team	Required

Using the development sequence and the feature weights as a guide, the planning team assigns classes to class owners.

Assign Major Feature Sets and Features to Chief Programmers	Planning Team	Required

Using the development sequence and the feature weights as a guide, the planning team assigns chief programmers as owners of feature sets.

Verification

Self Assessment	Planning Team	Required

Planning-team members, active in the process, provide internal self-assessment. External assessment is made on an as-needed basis, with senior management. Balance pure top-down planning by allowing developers an opportunity to assess the plan. Naturally, some developers are too conservative and want to extend a schedule. But, by contrast, project managers or chief programmers may tend to cast schedules in light of the "everyone is as capable as I am" syndrome. Or they may be trying to please stakeholders by being optimistic on a delivery date. Strike a balance.

Exit Criteria

To exit this process, the planning team must produce a development plan, subject to review and approval by the development manager and the chief architect:
- An overall completion date
- For each major feature set, feature set, and feature: its owner (CP) and its completion date
- For each class, its owner

Notes

We find that establishing a Future Features Board (FFB) accelerates feature prioritization. It also allows everyone else to play "good cops" and the FFB to play "bad cops." ("Sounds like a great feature. Let's see how the FFB prioritizes it.")

FDD Process #4: Design by Feature (DBF)

A chief programmer takes the next feature, identifies the classes likely to be involved, and contacts the corresponding class owners. This feature team works out a detailed sequence diagram. The class owners write class and method prologs. The team conducts a design inspection.

Entry Criteria
The planning team has successfully completed FDD Process #3, Plan by Feature.

Tasks

Form a DBF Team	Chief Programmer	Required

The chief programmer identifies the classes likely to be involved in the design of this feature. From the class ownership list, the chief programmer identifies the developers needed to form the feature team. He contacts those class owners, initiating the design of this feature. He contacts a domain member too, if he needs one to help design this feature.

Domain Walkthrough	Feature Team, Domain	Optional

(This task is optional, depending upon feature complexity.) The domain member gives an overview of the domain area for the feature under consideration. He includes domain information that is related to the feature but not necessarily a part of its implementation to help set context.

Study the Referenced Documents	Feature Team	Optional

(This task is optional, depending upon feature complexity.) Using referenced documents from the features list and any other pertinent documents they can get their hands on, the feature team studies the documents, extracting detailed supporting information about and for the feature.

Build a Sequence Diagram	Feature Team	Required

Applying their understanding of the feature, plus components and informal sequence diagrams, the feature team builds a formal, detailed sequence diagram for the feature. The team logs design alternatives, decisions, assumptions, and notes. The chief programmer adds the sequence diagram (and corresponding class-diagram updates, as is nearly always the case) to the project model.

Write Class and Method Prologs	Feature Team	Required

Each class owner updates his class and method prologs for his methods in the sequence diagram. He includes parameter types, return types, exceptions, and message sends.

Design Inspection	Feature Team	Required

The feature team conducts a design inspection. The chief programmer invites several people from outside the team to participate, when he feels the complexity of the feature warrants it.

Log Design-Inspection Action Items	Scribe	Required

A team scribe logs design-inspection action items for each class owner, for follow-up by that class owner.

Verification

Design Inspection	Feature Team	Required

The feature team walks through its sequence diagram(s) to provide an internal self-assessment. External assessment is made on an as-needed basis, to clarify functionality needs and scope.

Exit Criteria
To exit this process, the feature team must deliver the following results, subject to review and approval by the chief programmer (with oversight from the chief architect):
- The feature and its referenced documents (if any)
- The detailed sequence diagram
- Class-diagram updates
- Class and method prolog updates
- Notes on the team's consideration of significant design alternatives

FDD Process #5: Build By Feature (BBF)

Starting with a DBF package, each class owner builds his methods for the feature. He extends his class-based test cases and performs class-level (unit) testing. The feature team inspects the code, perhaps before unit test, as determined by the chief programmer. Once the code is successfully implemented and inspected, the class owner checks in his class(es) to the configuration management system. When all classes for this feature are checked in, the chief programmer promotes the code to the build process.

Entry Criteria

The feature team has successfully completed FDD Process #4, Design by Feature, for the features to be built during this DBF/BBF iteration.

Tasks

| Implement Classes and Methods | Feature Team | Required |

Each class owner implements the methods in support of this feature as specified in the detailed sequence diagram developed during DBF. He also adds test methods. The chief programmer adds end-to-end feature test methods.

| Code Inspection | Feature Team | Required |

The chief programmer schedules a BBF code inspection. (He might choose to do this before unit testing or after unit testing.) The feature team conducts a code inspection (with outside participants when the chief programmer sees the need for such participation).

| Log Code-Inspection Action Items | Scribe | Required |

A team scribe logs code-inspection action items for each class owner, for follow-up by that class owner.

| Unit Test | Feature Team | Required |

Each class owner tests his code and its support of the feature. The chief programmer, acting as the integration point for the entire feature, conducts end-to-end feature testing.

| Check in and Promote to the Build Process | Feature Team | Required |

Once the code is successfully implemented, inspected and tested, each class owner checks in his classes to the configuration management system. When all classes for the feature are checked in and shown to be working end-to-end, the chief programmer promotes the classes to the build process. The chief programmer updates the feature's status in the features list.

Verification

| Code Inspection and Unit Test | Feature Team | Required |

The features team conducts a code inspection. A team scribe logs action items for each class owner.

Exit Criteria

To exit this process, the feature team must deliver the following results, subject to review and approval by its chief programmer:
- Implemented and inspected methods and test methods
- Unit test results, for each method and for the overall sequence
- Classes checked in by owners, features promoted to the build process and updated by the chief programmer

6.6 CHIEF PROGRAMMERS, CLASS OWNERS, AND FEATURE TEAMS

In FDD, two roles are essential elements: chief programmers and class owners. And one sociological structure is key: feature teams. Let's take a closer look at these three.

6.6.1 Chief Programmer

Feature-driven development requires someone to lead the DBF/BBF processes, feature by feature, leading by example (as a designer and programmer) and by mentoring (especially by way of inspections).

The number of chief programmers limits how fast and how far you can go with your project. If you want to increase project speed, recruit another chief programmer. A chief programmer in this context is someone who is significantly more productive than others on your team. The amplifying factor comes from a combination of raw talent, skills, training, and experience. Occasionally all those talents come together within one human being.

Adding more programmers tends to slow down a project, as Fred Brooks observed decades ago. We find this to be true with one exception: with small, client-valued features and lightweight processes, when you add a chief programmer then you can add people around him and actually accelerate a project by increasing the amount of in-parallel development you can tackle—but again, only to a point.

6.6.2 Class Owner

A class owner is someone responsible for the design and implementation of a class. We find this works very effectively. First, developers gain a sense of ownership of some part of the code, and we find pride of ownership a good and motivating force. Second, it brings local consistency to a class (just one programmer touches the code).

The norm is one class, one class owner. Occasionally, for a class with algorithmically complex methods, you might need one class, one class owner, and one algorithm programmer.

Yet FDD organizes activities by feature, not by class. As it should. After all, FDD is all about producing frequent, tangible, working results—small, client-value features! *Clients use features.* They do not use the organizational framework that developers use to implement little pieces of a feature.

6.6.3 Feature Teams

We assign features to a chief programmer. He takes each feature and identifies the likely class owners who will be involved in delivering that feature. Then he forms a temporary, "lasts just a week or two" team, called a feature team (Figure 6-3).

Class owners work on more than one feature team at a time. Feature-team membership may change with each DBF/BBF iteration.

FIGURE 6-3. ▲ Feature-team membership may change with each DBF/BBF iteration.

FIGURE 6-4. ▲ Interactions within a feature team.

The chief programmer is just that, the chief! The interactions within the team are primarily between the chief programmer and the other team members (Figure 6-4). Why? We encourage this approach to accelerate progress, ensure on-going mentoring of the team members by the chief programmer, and promote uniformity of design and implementation.

Overall, the chief architect mentors the chief programmers, who in turn mentor the class owners within a feature team.

6.7 TRACKING PROGRESS WITH PRECISION

How much time do teams spend within each of the five processes of FDD? Here are some useful guidelines (Figure 6-5):

Develop an overall model.	10% initial, 4% ongoing
Build a features list.	4% initial, 1% ongoing
Plan by feature.	2% initial, 2% ongoing
Design by feature, build by feature.	77% (cycle time: every 2 weeks)

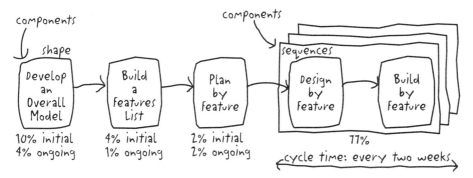

FIGURE 6-5. ▲ FDD processes with schedule percentages.

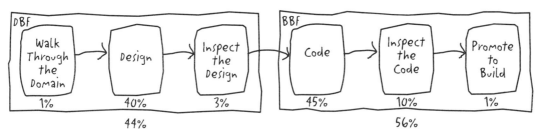

FIGURE 6-6. ▲ DBF/BBF milestone with schedule percentages.

Again, the percentages are useful guidelines (not absolutes).

The initial "develop an overall model, build a features list, and plan by feature" sequence consumes 16% of project schedule. The ongoing iterations of those front-end activities grab another 7%.

It's the other 77% we're concerned about in this section, the time spent in the many "design by feature, build by feature" iterations.

DBF/BBF consists of six little processes and corresponding schedule-percentage guidelines (Figure 6-6):

- DBF
    Walk through the domain.   1%
    Design.   40%
    Inspect the design.   3%
- BBF
    Code/test.   45%
    Inspect the code.   10%
    Promote to build.   1%

Note that the 45% for coding includes building unit-test methods and conducting units tests.

When applying DBF/BBF, do teams really spend less time designing (40% of DBF/BBF) than coding (45% of DBF/BBF)? Yes. Yet if we consider all of FDD and include initial object modeling when doing the comparison, we gain a bit more perspective on what is really happening here: Teams spend more time modeling and designing (45% of FDD) than coding (35% of FDD). The adage is still true: Succeed to plan, plan to succeed.

We plan for and track each DBF/BBF milestone. Remember that the total time from beginning to end is two weeks or less. So these milestones are very tiny—maybe "inch-pebbles."

The combination of small client-valued features and these six DBF/BBF milestones is the secret behind FDD's remarkable ability to track progress with precision.

Here's an example: For a given feature, once you've walked through the domain and designed the feature, you count that feature as 41% complete.

6.7.1 Reporting

The release manager meets weekly with the chief programmers. In this 30-minutes-or-less meeting, each chief programmer verbally walks through the status of his features, marking up the project-tracking chart as he goes. Doing this together, verbally, is a good way to make sure the chief programmers take time to listen to each other and are aware of where the others are at in the development process. At the end of the meeting, the release manager takes those results, updates the database, and generates reports.

The release manager issues progress reports weekly, for the team (Figure 6-7) and for clients and senior management (Figure 6-8).

For upper management and client reporting, we report the percentage complete for each major feature set and feature set on a monthly basis. In fact, we like to report progress visually. We draw rectangles for each major feature set, and then inside each rectangle we draw rectangles for each feature set. Then inside the inner rectangles, we show the feature-set name, a progress bar showing percent complete, and the planned completion month. See Figure 6-9.

Note that the symbol is in three sections. Each section has its own color-coding scheme. The upper section indicates overall status: work in progress (yellow), attention (red), completed (green), and not yet started (white). The middle section shows percent complete: percent complete (green). The lower section illustrates completion status: the targeted completion month, or completed (green). When a feature set is fully complete, the entire box turns green.

Figure 6-10 shows what this would look like in a project-wide view.

200 ▲

\<Major Feature-Set Name>.\<Feature-Set Name> (\<# of features>)

Id	Description	Chief Programmer	Class Owners	Walk-through		Design		Design Inspection		Development		Code Inspection		Promote to Build	
				Planned	Actual	Planned	Actual	Planned	Actual	Planned	Actual	Planned	Actual	Planned	Actual

Completion percentage for this feature set: __%

Expected completion month for this feature set: \<month> \<year>.

FIGURE 6-7. ▲ Feature tracking during DBF/BBF.

\<Major Feature-Set Name> (\<# of features>)

Feature Set (\<# of features>)	Total Features	Not Started	In Progress	Behind Schedule	Completed	Inactive	% Completed	Completion Date

FIGURE 6-8. ▲ Major feature set and feature set tracking during DBF/BBF (includes project-wide totals, too)

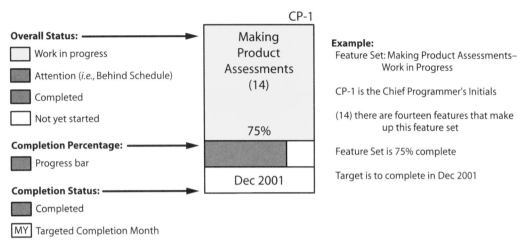

FIGURE 6-9. ▲ Reporting progress to upper management and clients.

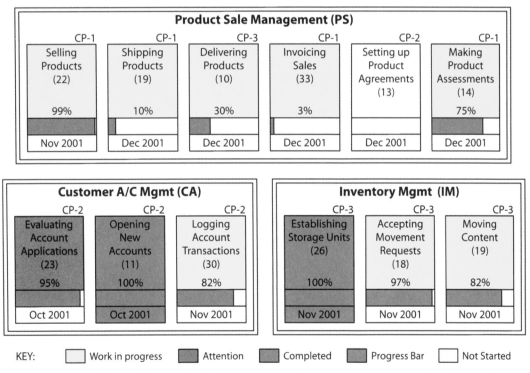

FIGURE 6-10. ▲ Reporting project-wide progress to upper management and clients.

6.7.2 Keeping a Features Database

Capture these items in your features database:

- Type (problem domain, human interaction, or system interaction)
- Identifier (feature-set prefix plus a sequence number)
- Status (on-hold, no longer required, normal)
- Major feature set
- Feature set
- Document references
- Action items
- Chief programmer
- Domain walk-through plan date, actual date
- Design plan date, actual date
- Design-inspection plan date, actual date
- Code plan date, actual date
- Code-inspection plan date, actual date
- Promote-to-build plan date, actual date
- Remarks

Track classes and owners in a separate table.
Automate reporting functions using your features database.

6.8 SUMMARY AND CONCLUSION

Feature-driven development is a process for helping teams produce frequent, tangible working results. It uses very small blocks of client-valued functionality, called features. FDD organizes those little blocks into business-related feature sets. FDD focuses developers on producing working results every two weeks. FDD includes planning strategies. And FDD tracks progress with precision.

We hope that you enjoy putting color archetypes, components, and feature-driven development to work on your projects. We wish you good success!

For ongoing news and updates, subscribe to The Coad Letter (a free series of special reports on better modeling and design, www.oi.com/publications.htm) and visit the Java Modeling home page (for additional components, updates, and more, www.oi.com/jm-book.htm).

Yours for better modeling and processes,

Peter Coad (pc@oi.com)

Eric Lefebvre (lefee@groupe-progestic.com)

Jeff De Luca (jdl@nebulon.com)

REFERENCES

[Brooks95] Brooks, Frederick P., Jr., *The Mythical Man Month: Essays on Software Engineering.* Anniversary Edition. Reading, MA: Addison Wesley, 1995.

[Davis98] Davis, Stan, and Christoper Meyer, *BLUR: The Speed of Change in the Connected Economy.* Reading, MA: Perseus Books, 1998.

A

Archetypes in Color

This appendix is an "archetype in color summary.
Figure A-1 presents archetypes in color.
Figure A-2 presents the domain-neutral component.

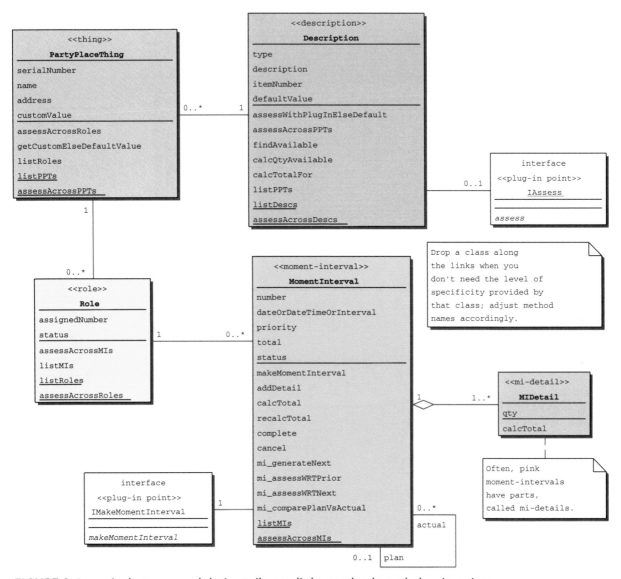

FIGURE A-1. ▲ Archetypes and their attributes, links, methods, and plug-in points.

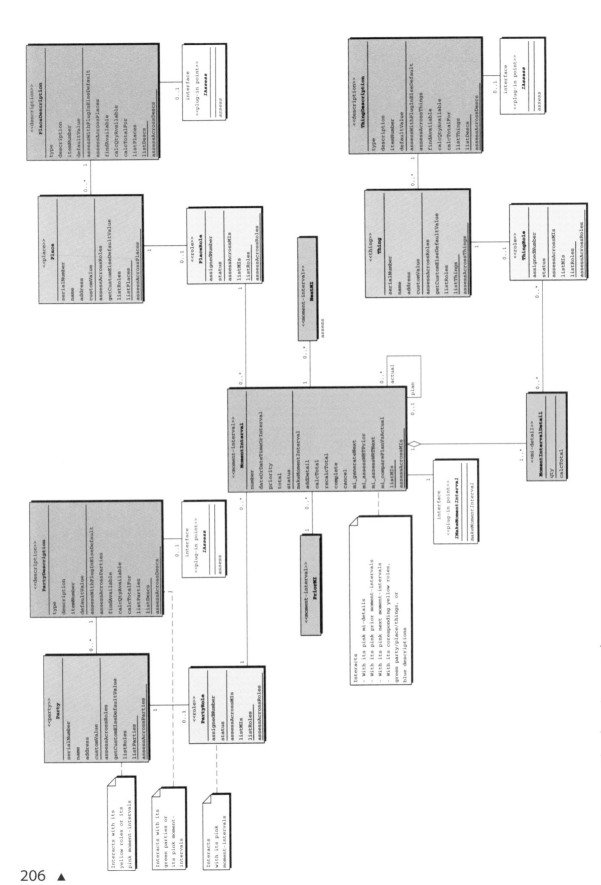

FIGURE A-2. ▲ The domain-neutral component.

B Modeling Tips

We present a series of modeling tips in Chapters 2–5. Each time, we teach by example, then summarize with a tip. Once we cover a tip, we do not repeat it in subsequent material. So Chapter 2 has the most tips.

Realizing that you might choose to read this book in any number of ways, we list all of the tips here in one place, for your convenience.

From Chapter 2

Tip. Green or blue? Use green party/place/thing when it's uniquely identifiable and you need to track it that way. Otherwise, use some quantity of a blue description instead. (Section 2.1.1)

Tip. Validate then do? Merge into a single step for the sender, passing arguments and letting the receiver encapsulate all steps in the process. The receiver validates, performs the requested action, and returns the result to the sender. (Section 2.1.1)

Tip. Values from an object several links away? Ask for the object, then ask it for the values you need. Don't pass the command through several layers of intermediaries, unless that command is useful to the intermediary objects as well. (Section 2.1.1)

Tip. Yellow role with no added responsibilities? Express that yellow role with a text label rather than with another yellow role. (Section 2.1.2)

Tip. Association or aggregation? Association is by far the norm, the 90 percent case. Use aggregation only when you want to give the added meaning of whole-part, container-content, or group-member. (Section 2.1.2)

Tip. Notable subsets? If you want to show that an association or aggregation link has notable subsets, use a qualifier label and list what those subsets are. For example: "all, accepted." Implement a separate member for each collection you list. (Section 2.1.3)

Tip. Repeatedly asking for state? If you find an object repeatedly asking objects it links to what state they are in, let the object hold state-specific collections. That simplifies the design and reduces message traffic. (Section 2.1.3)

Tip. Where to put a method? Take a feature statement, <action> the <result> <by|for|of|to> a <moment-interval | role| description | party, place, thing>. Put the initiating method in the corresponding class. (Section 2.1.3)

Tip. Calculate and recalculate? Begin with a calculate method. Add a buffered result attribute if values or plug-in algorithms might change on you, affecting the result of the calculation. Add a recalculate method if you need a way to force recalculation (ignoring any buffered value). (Section 2.1.3)

Tip. Add extra associations? Add extra associations to simplify frequent object interactions that would otherwise traverse across a number of intermediary objects (simpler design, simpler implementation). (Section 2.1.6)

Tip. Common functionality? If small, don't factor it out. If larger, consider using domain-based inheritance or algorithm plug-in points. (Section 2.1.7)

Tip. When to use inheritance? Use inheritance to express specialized moment-intervals, descriptions, or party/place/things. (Section 2.2.1)

Tip. When not to use inheritance? Not for "is a role played by a" (use a yellow role instead). Not for changes of what you know about something over time (use pink moment-intervals to show that progression). Not to factor out an algorithm (use a plug-in point instead). (Section 2.2.1)

Tip. Class name hidden as an attribute name or within an attribute name? Move it out to its own class, if the added capability is within your scope. (Section 2.2.1)

Tip. Derivable link? Sometimes you'd like to show a link from class A to class B, even though that link is derivable by following two or more required links from B back to A. This often happens when modeling yellow roles and a sequence of pink moment-intervals. Show the extra link. Label it "derivable" so others know the link is for model expressiveness (not necessarily for implementation). (Section 2.2.3)

Tip. Behavior across a collection? Use class methods to express behavior across the collection of all of the objects in a class. Use problem-domain objects to express behavior across the collection of objects it links to. Rarely needed: add another class, a "pool" class, to express behavior across some other collection. (Section 2.2.4)

Tip.   Series of aggregation links? Try modeling the upper-level classes in the series as a single class, with an aggregation link connecting one object to others in the same class. Use a sequence diagram to show how it works. This approach often simplifies a model without any loss of expressiveness. (Section 2.3.2)

Tip.   Template, plan, then actual? Model with one template class and one plan/actual class. Link a template to plans, the each plan to actual(s). Label the link ends "plan 0..1" and "actual 0..*." (Section 2.3.3)

Tip.   Compare two objects with each other? Better: let one of the two compare itself to the other. This keeps related things together and makes reuse much more likely. (Section 2.3.3)

Tip.   Interacting with another system or a device? Model a logical class (a problem-domain boundary for your system) and a physical proxy class (a system-interaction class). (Section 2.3.4)

Tip.   Polling within your model? No. Let your objects do their own things, reporting only as needed. (A physical-device proxy polls a physical if it needs it.) (Section 2.3.4)

From Chapter 3

Tip.   An attribute? Or something more? If you need an attribute value, use an attribute. If you need to track the change in that value over time (past, present, future), use a pink moment-interval. If you need to set that value once and then apply it to other objects as a standard, use a blue description. (Section 3.1.1)

Tip.   Track values for each link? Add a pink moment-interval. Just need to categorize links? Use this simpler approach: label the endpoint of the link with the categories. (Section 3.1.1)

Tip.   Track different versions? Make a copy, copy its parts, and link the original to the copy. After that, use a "diff" (difference) method to identify what has changed. Alternative: keep the original and track each change (sometimes simpler). (Section 3.1.5)

Tip.   A link from first to last? If a class links to another, and that one links to another, do you need a link from the first to the last? If the first and the last need to and can associate with each other even without the middle, yes. If not, no (although you could add it and label it "derivable" if it helps in understanding the model). (Section 3.2.1)

Tip.   Complex method in a sequence-diagram column? Break the method down into smaller steps (using messages that point back to the same object; UML calls them self-delegation messages). Then work out dynamics for each step. (Section 3.2.2)

Tip. Objects linked to a pink moment-interval change over time? If so, add attributes to "snapshot" the objects you need to remember. (Section 3.3)

Tip. Send a message from one role to another? Two paths: go through a pink moment-interval. Or if the roles are played by the same person, place, or thing, then go through the common green one instead. (Section 3.3)

From Chapter 4

Tip. Link to a description and an "at this level" description? Link first to the "at this level" description; let the "at this level" description link to the description itself. (Section 4.1.2)

Tip. Transform inheritance (kinds of) into composition (parts of)? Nearly always, the result is more flexible. Do not use inheritance to factor out a common function (use composition and a plug-in point instead). (Section 4.1.4)

Tip. Groupings of roles or groupings of parties? Use groupings of roles rather than groupings of parties. This lets you work with groupings without affecting the parties involved. For example, an applicant group for a loan is just that: a group of applicants (a group of applicant-role objects, that is). (Section 4.2.1)

From Chapter 5

Tip. Activate, deactivate, and monitor? Use activate/deactivate and monitor methods to express initial activation followed by some on-going behavior, running asynchronously over some period of time. (Section 5.1.1)

Tip. Plan then actual? Model with one class. Link each plan to actual(s). Label the link ends "plan 0..1" and "actual 0..*". (Section 5.1.2)

Tip. A pink moment-interval object with at most one corresponding subsequent moment-interval object? Consider merging the two, resulting in a simpler overall model. (Section 5.3.2)

Notation

This appendix is a notation summary.

Figure C-1 presents class-diagram notation and conventions.

Figure C-2 presents sequence-diagram notation and conventions.

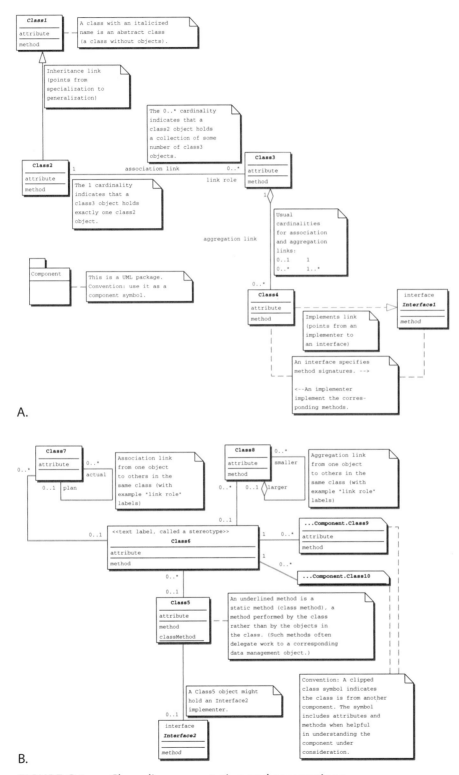

A.

B.

FIGURE C-1 ▲ Class-diagram notation and conventions.

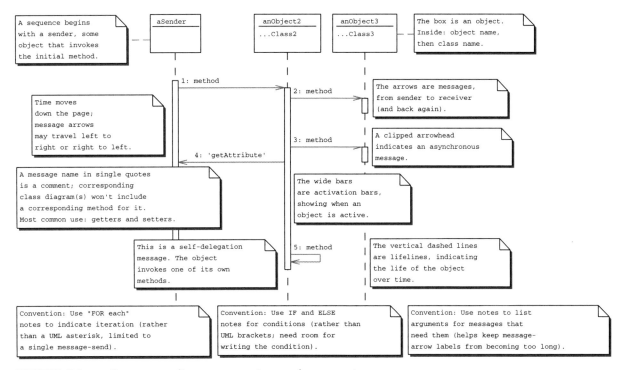

FIGURE C-2. ▲ Sequence-diagram notation and conventions.

Index

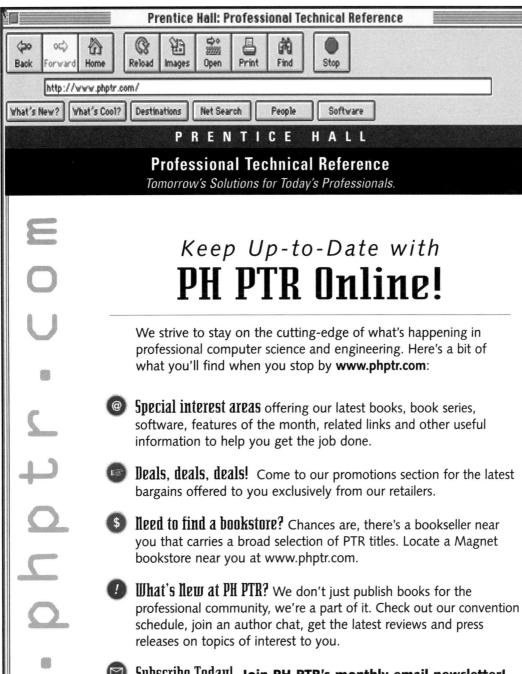

LICENSE AGREEMENT AND LIMITED WARRANTY

READ THE FOLLOWING TERMS AND CONDITIONS CAREFULLY BEFORE OPENING THIS CD PACKAGE. THIS LEGAL DOCUMENT IS AN AGREEMENT BETWEEN YOU AND PRENTICE-HALL, INC. (THE "COMPANY"). BY OPENING THIS SEALED CD PACKAGE, YOU ARE AGREEING TO BE BOUND BY THESE TERMS AND CONDITIONS. IF YOU DO NOT AGREE WITH THESE TERMS AND CONDITIONS, DO NOT OPEN THE CD PACKAGE. PROMPTLY RETURN THE UNOPENED CD PACKAGE AND ALL ACCOMPANYING ITEMS TO THE PLACE YOU OBTAINED THEM FOR A FULL REFUND OF ANY SUMS YOU HAVE PAID.

1.   **GRANT OF LICENSE:** In consideration of your purchase of this book, and your agreement to abide by the terms and conditions of this Agreement, the Company grants to you a nonexclusive right to use and display the copy of the enclosed software program (hereinafter the "SOFTWARE") on a single computer (i.e., with a single CPU) at a single location so long as you comply with the terms of this Agreement. The Company reserves all rights not expressly granted to you under this Agreement.

2.   **OWNERSHIP OF SOFTWARE:** You own only the magnetic or physical media (the enclosed CD) on which the SOFTWARE is recorded or fixed, but the Company and the software developers retain all the rights, title, and ownership to the SOFTWARE recorded on the original CD copy(ies) and all subsequent copies of the SOFTWARE, regardless of the form or media on which the original or other copies may exist. This license is not a sale of the original SOFTWARE or any copy to you.

3.   **COPY RESTRICTIONS:** This SOFTWARE and the accompanying printed materials and user manual (the "Documentation") are the subject of copyright. The individual programs on the CD are copyrighted by the authors of each program. Some of the programs on the CD include separate licensing agreements. If you intend to use one of these programs, you must read and follow its accompanying license agreement. You may not copy the Documentation or the SOFTWARE, except that you may make a single copy of the SOFTWARE for backup or archival purposes only. You may be held legally responsible for any copying or copyright infringement which is caused or encouraged by your failure to abide by the terms of this restriction.

4.   **USE RESTRICTIONS:** You may not network the SOFTWARE or otherwise use it on more than one computer or computer terminal at the same time. You may physically transfer the SOFTWARE from one computer to another provided that the SOFTWARE is used on only one computer at a time. You may not distribute copies of the SOFTWARE or Documentation to others. You may not reverse engineer, disassemble, decompile, modify, adapt, translate, or create derivative works based on the SOFTWARE or the Documentation without the prior written consent of the Company.

5.   **TRANSFER RESTRICTIONS:** The enclosed SOFTWARE is licensed only to you and may not be transferred to any one else without the prior written consent of the Company. Any unauthorized transfer of the SOFTWARE shall result in the immediate termination of this Agreement.

6.   **TERMINATION:** This license is effective until terminated. This license will terminate automatically without notice from the Company and become null and void if you fail to comply with any provisions or limitations of this license. Upon termination, you shall destroy the Documentation and all copies of the SOFTWARE. All provisions of this Agreement as to warranties, limitation of liability, remedies or damages, and our ownership rights shall survive termination.

7.   **MISCELLANEOUS:** This Agreement shall be construed in accordance with the laws of the United States of America and the State of New York and shall benefit the Company, its affiliates, and assignees.

8.   **LIMITED WARRANTY AND DISCLAIMER OF WARRANTY:** The Company warrants that the SOFTWARE, when properly used in accordance with the Documentation, will operate in substantial conformity with the description of the SOFTWARE set forth in the Documentation. The Company does not warrant that the SOFTWARE will meet your requirements or that the operation

of the SOFTWARE will be uninterrupted or error-free. The Company warrants that the media on which the SOFTWARE is delivered shall be free from defects in materials and workmanship under normal use for a period of thirty (30) days from the date of your purchase. Your only remedy and the Company's only obligation under these limited warranties is, at the Company's option, return of the warranted item for a refund of any amounts paid by you or replacement of the item. Any replacement of SOFTWARE or media under the warranties shall not extend the original warranty period. The limited warranty set forth above shall not apply to any SOFTWARE which the Company determines in good faith has been subject to misuse, neglect, improper installation, repair, alteration, or damage by you. EXCEPT FOR THE EXPRESSED WARRANTIES SET FORTH ABOVE, THE COMPANY DISCLAIMS ALL WARRANTIES, EXPRESS OR IMPLIED, INCLUDING WITHOUT LIMITATION, THE IMPLIED WARRANTIES OF MERCHANTABILITY AND FITNESS FOR A PARTICULAR PURPOSE. EXCEPT FOR THE EXPRESS WARRANTY SET FORTH ABOVE, THE COMPANY DOES NOT WARRANT, GUARANTEE, OR MAKE ANY REPRESENTATION REGARDING THE USE OR THE RESULTS OF THE USE OF THE SOFTWARE IN TERMS OF ITS CORRECTNESS, ACCURACY, RELIABILITY, CURRENTNESS, OR OTHERWISE.

IN NO EVENT, SHALL THE COMPANY OR ITS EMPLOYEES, AGENTS, SUPPLIERS, OR CONTRACTORS BE LIABLE FOR ANY INCIDENTAL, INDIRECT, SPECIAL, OR CONSEQUENTIAL DAMAGES ARISING OUT OF OR IN CONNECTION WITH THE LICENSE GRANTED UNDER THIS AGREEMENT, OR FOR LOSS OF USE, LOSS OF DATA, LOSS OF INCOME OR PROFIT, OR OTHER LOSSES, SUSTAINED AS A RESULT OF INJURY TO ANY PERSON, OR LOSS OF OR DAMAGE TO PROPERTY, OR CLAIMS OF THIRD PARTIES, EVEN IF THE COMPANY OR AN AUTHORIZED REPRESENTATIVE OF THE COMPANY HAS BEEN ADVISED OF THE POSSIBILITY OF SUCH DAMAGES. IN NO EVENT SHALL LIABILITY OF THE COMPANY FOR DAMAGES WITH RESPECT TO THE SOFTWARE EXCEED THE AMOUNTS ACTUALLY PAID BY YOU, IF ANY, FOR THE SOFTWARE.

SOME JURISDICTIONS DO NOT ALLOW THE LIMITATION OF IMPLIED WARRANTIES OR LIABILITY FOR INCIDENTAL, INDIRECT, SPECIAL, OR CONSEQUENTIAL DAMAGES, SO THE ABOVE LIMITATIONS MAY NOT ALWAYS APPLY. THE WARRANTIES IN THIS AGREEMENT GIVE YOU SPECIFIC LEGAL RIGHTS AND YOU MAY ALSO HAVE OTHER RIGHTS WHICH VARY IN ACCORDANCE WITH LOCAL LAW.

ACKNOWLEDGMENT

YOU ACKNOWLEDGE THAT YOU HAVE READ THIS AGREEMENT, UNDERSTAND IT, AND AGREE TO BE BOUND BY ITS TERMS AND CONDITIONS. YOU ALSO AGREE THAT THIS AGREEMENT IS THE COMPLETE AND EXCLUSIVE STATEMENT OF THE AGREEMENT BETWEEN YOU AND THE COMPANY AND SUPERSEDES ALL PROPOSALS OR PRIOR AGREEMENTS, ORAL, OR WRITTEN, AND ANY OTHER COMMUNICATIONS BETWEEN YOU AND THE COMPANY OR ANY REPRESENTATIVE OF THE COMPANY RELATING TO THE SUBJECT MATTER OF THIS AGREEMENT.

Should you have any questions concerning this Agreement or if you wish to contact the Company for any reason, please contact in writing at the address below.

Robin Short

Prentice Hall PTR

One Lake Street

Upper Saddle River, New Jersey 07458

About the CD-ROM

The Software Included on the CD-ROM will help you really master
Java™ modeling

We wanted to deliver more than just a book. You see, no matter how good any book is, nothing replaces the added understanding and insights that come from hands-on experience. So to help you get the most out of your Java modeling experience, to make it more hands-on and more effective, we've put together this special Java Modeling CD-ROM. It features:

• Together®J Whiteboard Edition (no time limits, no size limits)
• Models and Java source code (61 components, 283 classes, 46 interfaces, 671 attributes, 1139 methods, and 65 interaction sequences)
• Multiframe HTML documentation
• Modeling tips

Buy the book. Start reading. Install the software and take it for a spin. View and edit the source code using TJ's "simultaneous" round-trip engineering. View the sequence diagrams too. Keep reading. And applying.

THEN use your new Java modeling skills and the software to design and build better apps. You're on your way!

THIS IS A MULTIPLATFORM CD
Use it on Windows® 95/98/NT®, Solaris™, Linux, and OS/2®.

FOR MORE INFORMATION
Visit http://www.oi.com/jm-book.htm

TECHNICAL SUPPORT
If you have a problem with the CBT software, please contact CBT Technical Support. In the U.S., call 1-800-938-3247. If you are outside the U.S., call 3531-283-0380.

Prentice Hall does not offer technical support for this software. However, if there is a problem with the media, you may obtain a replacement copy by e-mailing us with your problem at:
disc_exchange@prenhall.com